MGA

Osprey AutoHistory

MGA

1500, 1600, Twin Cam

F. WILSON McCOMB

Published in 1983 by Osprey Publishing Limited
12–14 Long Acre, London WC2E 9LP
Member company of the George Philip Group

Sole distributors for the USA

British Library Cataloguing in Publication Data

McComb, Wilson F.
MGA.—(Autohistory)
1. M.G. automobile
I. Title II. Series
629.2'222 TL215.M5
ISBN 0-85045-499-9

Editor Tim Parker
Associate Michael Sedgwick
Picture research by the author
Design Trevor Verdigan

Filmset in Great Britain
Printed in Spain

Contents

Preface

Captain George Eyston, OBE, MC, MA, was a man possessed of such boundless enthusiasm and energy that for the greater part of his four-score years he left ordinary folk breathless in the vain attempt to keep up with him. He raced motorcycles under an assumed name while still a schoolboy, and gained the Land Speed Record three times at more than 300 mph. He was a yachtsman of Olympic standard and held a pilot's licence until the age of 70. He secured his first MG record in 1930, his last in 1954, and continued to direct all MG record attempts including the last, in 1959.

Becoming President of the MG Car Club, he took his duties seriously, as one would expect of such an individual, but I still cannot imagine how he found time to arrange for the Club's general secretary to do a tour of the American MG clubs in 1965. For me it meant that inside 30 days I crossed the Atlantic twice, travelled 13,000 miles within the States by road or air, attended the New York Auto Show and the Sebring 12 Hours Race, and stayed in more than a score of hotels from Boston to Tampa to Seattle to San Diego. Eventually I managed to return all the room keys I'd forgotten to hand in, but it took a while.

So, however hard I try, I cannot now recall where it was that I sat in an American hotel bar talking to

one of the local MG salesmen when, somehow, the conversation turned to the MGA—then out of production by more than two years. I certainly remember the salesman's exact words. 'The MGA?' he said. 'Man, that was a *nothing* automobile'.

It was late and I was too tired to argue with the fellow, who probably believed that selling MGs was no different from selling Pontiacs or Buicks or soap powder. I didn't point out that the MGA had been the marque's first major break with tradition in more than 30 years, and a change that the world's motoring press had greeted with unanimous approval; that its commercial success was immediate

Far Left *Capt George Eyston at the Twin Cam press preview, 1958*

Above *MGAs check out of Abingdon for road delivery to Southampton. When this picture was taken, 1500 cars a month were going to the US importers, Hambro Automotive Corporation Inc*

and spectacular, the annual production of MG sports cars leaping from the TF's 1954 peak of 6520 cars to the MGA's 20,571 in 1957, thus saving the Company from probable extinction; that MGA total production—101,081 cars in seven years—was a world record in its time, and more than double the entire output of TCs, TDs and TFs in a decade; that more than 94 per cent of all MGAs built had been exported, the vast majority of them to his country; that the MGA had expanded Abingdon's sports car market far beyond the confines of the 'square-riggers', and thus paved the way for the still greater success of the MGB.

Nor did I mention (and I'm sure it would not have interested him) that the Abingdon design office had been closed down when the MG Car Company was sold to Morris Motors in 1935, and stayed that way—apart from a tiny drafting team to handle odd jobs—until the middle of 1954. Which meant that the entire T type series beloved by MG traditionalists, from TA to TF inclusive, had in fact been designed at Cowley, Oxford. Which in turn meant that the MGA was the first MG in 20-odd years to be designed *as* an MG, by an MG design team located at Abingdon and headed by MG's own chief engineer. On that basis it was most emphatically not a streamlined substitute for the real thing, as so many dyed-in-the-wool enthusiasts believed, but a true MG with a better pedigree than the cars they held so dear.

And finally, I didn't attempt to tell him what it felt like to get into a well-set-up MGA and drive it just as hard as one was capable of doing, over a winding, swooping stretch of gloriously open country road, or on the banked track at Montlhéry, or Brands Hatch, or the Club circuit at Silverstone. He wouldn't have understood what in hell I was talking about. But I knew, and I can still remember the joy of it.

Chapter 1
T-time was over

The square-rigged traditional MG two-seater has been an object of affection among sports car fans for so long now that its shape exists in a sort of vacuum. It has this curious aura of timelessness which seems to make comparisons not merely odious, but irrelevant, and precludes adverse criticism. To offer any disparaging comment nowadays is about as popular as suggesting, say, that a new Royal baby is a squint-eyed, squalling little horror. It is Not Done.

But it *was* done 30-odd years ago. In the early 1950s the T series MGs were increasingly looked on as unfortunate, anachronistic survivals in a developing modern world. A 1951 issue of the weekly *Autosport* lists a selection of cars marketed in sports, drophead or convertible coupé form which laid claim to high performance, or at least 'sporting' characteristics. They were AC, Allard, Alvis, Armstrong-Siddeley, Aston Martin, Austin A40 Sports, Connaught, Delahaye, Ferrari, Fiat, Frazer-Nash, Healey, HRG, Jaguar, Jensen, Jowett, Lea-Francis, Marauder, MG, Morgan, Panhard, Simca and Sunbeam Alpine (but not Triumph, which had briefly disappeared from the scene before re-emerging as the TR2).

Of these two dozen cars, all but four had either full-width bodywork or a well-smoothed shell of racing ancestry. Only three—HRG, MG and

This handsome drophead coupé, built in Switzerland, was one of many attempts to modernize the TD

Morgan—could truly be described as traditional square-riggers, with the Singer Roadster hovering uncertainly in the middle, looking like a Y type tourer that had lost its way in Warwickshire. Morgan, as always, were a law unto themselves because they could survive on a production level of backyard proportions. HRG were fast fading out of active manufacture.

So there was reason for concern, even though the T types were still commercially successful. As everyone knows, the TC and TD sold exceptionally well overseas—so well, indeed, that only a handful remained behind for home consumption; in 1952, for example, a mere 246 TDs were available for sale in the UK out of 10,838 built that year. The lucky British buyer who acquired a new MG during the post-WW2 period could keep it for the minimum two years stipulated by government regulations, then sell it for at least twice the car's original price.

Though less shapely, this American-designed fibreglass TD caught the attention of Colonel Goldie Gardner, who sent a picture to John Thornley with approving comment

When criticism of the MGs was heard at home—which it was—it came mostly from theorists who were themselves driving around in pre-war cars. Most of us were, of necessity, until the 'covenant' rule was relaxed in January 1953.

Overseas, where buyers were free to pick and choose, it was a different story. As early as 1947, Abingdon received *via* Nuffield Exports Ltd an inquiry from a Beverly Hills dealer: could he please have a quotation for supplying 70 drive-away Y type chassis? They were to be shipped without fenders (wings) or radiator case, with radiator block lowered and steering column lengthened (in each case, by four inches), TC exhaust manifold, TC remote-control assembly, TC generator and tachometer, 4:1 final drive instead of 5.143, and each engine fitted with a supercharger—which he would supply. It was stated that on arrival in California the chassis would be fitted with Italian bodywork.

Abingdon quoted a modest £211 per chassis (the retail price of a Y type saloon, less tax, was then £525). But nothing came of the idea, and within a year the Nuffield Organization tried rather unsuccessfully to market its own Y type tourer overseas. In 1952 'Wacky' Arnolt's substantial Arnolt Corporation of Warsaw, Indiana, made a somewhat similar approach regarding TD chassis, and asked Bertone to design two bodies: a handsome close-coupled four-seater convertible and what Wacky called a 'saloon coupe' (without the acute accent, naturally). It was said that these weighed only 20 and 40 lb more, respectively, than the stock TD. Such a small weight increase is a little hard to believe, and Arnolt soon switched his

Strictly functional, Dick Jacobs' fibreglass coupé on the last YB chassis was raced in 1954. A full-width open car on a TD chassis was also built for one of his customers

Ex-Wolseley apprentice Ken Miles, the service manager of Gough Industries Inc in California, won many awards with his way-out T-type special. Later he drove EX 179 at Utah in 1954 and 1956

attention to the 2-litre Bristol chassis instead.

Other overseas dealers or importers also experimented with the TD, either fitting complete new fibreglass bodies or merely tarting up the ordinary car by means of two-tone paint jobs, special road wheels, steering wheels, wind wings, fancy tonneau covers and matching spare wheel covers, central armrests, locking tops for the luggage space, hardtops—just about anything, in fact, to make the TD look somewhat less Olde Worlde Abingdonian. As Roger Barlow of Beverly Hills had realized five years earlier, it was easy enough to sell Clark Gable and others a TC when the square-rigged shape seemed novel and cute to the Hollywood community, but once they had laid eyes on the sort of sports car that Italian stylists produced, angularity suddenly lost its charm.

Then there were the racing enthusiasts to consider. True, only a tiny proportion of MG buyers actually raced their cars, but it is a basic fact of life that sports car buyers demand a great deal more performance than most of them will ever actually use; any Sunday morning in England, lounge bars

Above *George Phillips (better known as 'Phil') raced his rebodied TC not only in Britain, but also at Le Mans and Comminges in France*

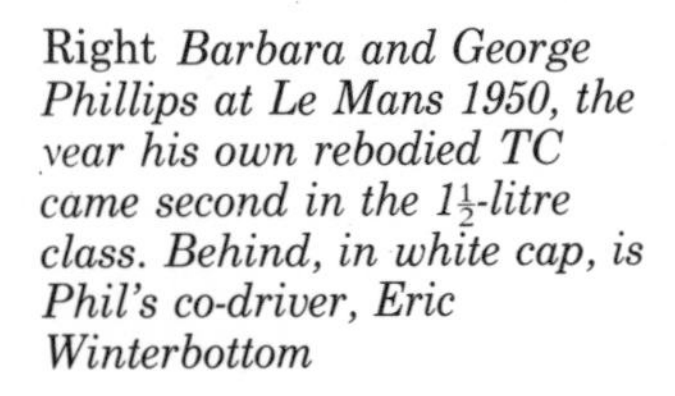

Right *Barbara and George Phillips at Le Mans 1950, the year his own rebodied TC came second in the 1½-litre class. Behind, in white cap, is Phil's co-driver, Eric Winterbottom*

echo to the boasting of check-capped individuals who may never break a speed limit. Moreover, racing successes really do play their part in enhancing a marque's reputation.

So far as the T series MGs were concerned, the racing fraternity retained their well-founded respect for the seemingly unbreakable XPAG (1250 cc) and XPEG (1466 cc) engines, but usually threw the rest of the car away if they wanted real performance. Cooper, Kieft, Lester, Lister, Lotus, Tojeiro—all these and more were built as successful sports-racing machines with T series MG engines, but their chassis owed nothing to Abingdon. A notable example is the Mark IX Lotus-MG 1500. It weighed just over 1000 lb—exactly half as much as a TF 1500. Its low-drag bodywork, scarcely in the 'shopping' category, obviously presented far less frontal area, and it pulled a final drive ratio of 3.66:1 instead of 4.88. With engine tuned to give 85 bhp at 5800 rpm, well within the capabilities of the XPEG unit (which had a power peak of 63 bhp at 5500 in production form), the Lotus-MG had a maximum speed of 128.6 mph, exactly 50 per cent more than that of the TF 1500, and accelerated from 0 to 60 mph in 8.6 sec—exactly half the time taken by the Abingdon car.

Some folk went to extraordinary lengths to drag more power from the unfortunate T series engine. Following the factory's own tuning stages, the 1250 cc unit could be persuaded to give a reasonably impressive 97.5 bhp at 6000 rpm with 9.3:1 compression ratio and Shorrock supercharger. An American MG enthusiast named John Edgar reckoned he could do better. He dropped the geometric compression ratio to 6:1 by fitting a thick copper gasket, employed high-tensile head studs, a special high-lift camshaft and stupendous 220 lb valve springs. The bottom end remained standard except for tougher big-end bolts. Edgar's demoniac tweak was an

In the 1950 Production Car Race at Silverstone, the archaic appearance of Ted Lund's works TD is emphasized by Ascari's Tipo 166 Ferrari

Italmeccanica supercharger running at 12,000 rpm and giving 12 psi boost. With this he claimed a peak of 148 bhp at undisclosed rpm, which is a specific output of 118.4 bhp/litre—remarkable indeed for a simple pushrod ohv engine. To keep the whole thing from blowing sky-high he had to use pure ethylene glycol as the coolant instead of water, and needed an intercooler to hold down the charge temperature between supercharger and induction tract. For this the coolant was ordinary water, but in addition to passing through a sidemounted radiator it flowed around a floormounted tank filled with solid carbon dioxide.

Lacking the usual 'eggbox' grille, Archie Craig's Cooper-MG has a more Maserati-like air

As John Edgar's use of dry ice suggests, these are misty regions indeed for the designer of an inexpensive production sports car like the MG. Yet the whole future policy of Abingdon was influenced by the way these enthusiasts strove to force their T types through the atmosphere regardless of the fact that, in John Thornley's words, the resistance curve of such bodywork makes it 'almost as impenetrable as a brick wall' at around 85 mph. As is now common knowledge, the production MGA was derived directly from a special-bodied TD that the factory built for a private individual, George Phillips, to drive at Le Mans in 1951.

T.D. for Le Mans. — Phillips

1. ? Lighter Gauge Chassis or Extensive lightening — Last year – wet – 3 galls. 12¼ cwt.

2. Al-fin brake drums.

3. Motor set back 2" & down 2" ?

4. TC Gearbox

5. Overall ratio 18.5 mph per 1000.

6. ~~30~~ 24 Gallon tank.

7. 80 Octane fuel ∴ TT Engine

8. Special sump — J.W.T.

9. Exhaust pipe to clear sump.

10. Body – à la G.E.P. special or 'all-over' ? Walter White.

11. Instruments. Rev Ctr. Ammeter. Oil Press. Water thermo.

T.C. Weighed at Abingdon – 12 Galls & tools – 14-0-14 lbs.

12. Can we do Ms Andrea ?

Mille Miglia ? ~~April~~
Le Mans. 22/23 June
Spa ? July.
Nurburg 24 Aug/Sept.

13½

Accounts of the 1951 Le Mans race are contradictory: some say the fuel supplied was so poor that it caused detonation and damage; some pointed out that when the MG dropped one of its large-diameter Mark II valves, it was by no means the first to do so; some said bluntly that Phil had pressed the car too hard. Whatever the truth of the matter, he certainly showed what UMG 400 could do with its handsome bodywork and quite mildly-tuned 1250 cc

Above *Roy Brocklehurst, now one of the leading backroom boys in BL Technology Ltd, was only 20 when he designed the special EX 175 and EX 179 chassis frame for Syd Enever*

engine, which made it the smallest-capacity British car in the race.

Phil's *standing* lap was timed at close on 72 mph, which exceeded by more than 10 mph his set average speed for the race. Whistling through the Mulsanne flying kilometre at 116 mph, he was soon lapping at over 80, and on his 29th lap recorded 83.6 mph. This was nothing like as fast as the 1500 cc Gordini-entered Simcas, of which the Trintignant/Behra car lapped at 94 mph, but all four of them blew up. Unfortunately so did the MG, after 60 laps, leaving the slower Becquart/Wilkins Jowett Jupiter as sole survivor—and winner— of the 1500 cc class. When I asked Phil about it later, he merely remarked that MG valves were 'made of bloody park railings'.

Although UMG 400 had failed at Le Mans, Syd Enever remained intrigued by the possibilities of this rebodied TD. The shape—so different from that of the angular production car—had been much admired, but the seating position was too high because of the narrow TD chassis frame. Otherwise, Enever felt sure, it had the makings of a good road car.

As mentioned earlier, MG's design set-up was very peculiar. Shortly after designing the brilliantly-advanced R-type single-seater of 1935, H. N. Charles had been transferred to Cowley following the Morris Motors takeover. For a man who liked independent suspension and high-output ohc engines, the new pushrod ohv MG range held little interest, and he soon decided to leave. About the same time, a young man named Gerald Palmer approached Cecil Kimber, having designed rather an attractive sports car, the Deroy, which had not gone into production. Kimber recommended him to Cowley, where Palmer worked on various things, including the car that eventually appeared in 1947 as the Y type MG saloon—whose chassis later formed the basis of the TD.

EX 179 is tested on the MIRA banked track. This successful record car used the spare wide-type chassis, TF1500 engine, and a near-replica of the Gardner-MG bodywork

Then the story starts to get complicated. In 1942 Gerry Palmer moved to Jowett, there to earn fame as designer of the much-praised Jowett Javelin saloon (but not the Jupiter sports car, which was mainly the work of Professor Eberan von Eberhorst). However, the Javelin had barely got into full production when Palmer moved back to Cowley again with instructions to design new cars for MG and Riley—both of which marques were then built at Abingdon. Meanwhile Syd Enever, who had remained at Abingdon when the design

Rival project: Gerry Palmer produced an alternative design at Cowley while the MGA was taking shape at Abingdon. As a monocoque, the Palmer car was lighter, but lacked the extensive testing of EX 175 and EX 179

office was transferred to Cowley, had in 1947 hired a bright young design apprentice called Roy Brocklehurst to help with some of the odd jobs that came his way. Enever did this out of a small annual budget which enabled him to buy labour but precluded capital expenditure, and as Roy Brocklehurst put it to me, so long as Syd kept within that budget, 'nobody cared whether he took on 14 chimps or two PhDs'.

Roy would be the first to admit that initially he belonged more in the chimp category, for he was straight out of school, only 15, and laboriously learning his engineering theory at evening classes. But he soon found himself drawing special crankshafts and valve gear for the Gardner-MG record car, and when Enever decided to rework the Phillips Le Mans car, he gave young Roy the job of designing a new and wider chassis frame which would allow the occupants to sit lower down between side-members and transmission tunnel. By the time 20-year-old Roy Brocklehurst departed in June 1952 for his deferred two-year period of National Service with the RAF, this chassis design had been completed.

From Gerry Palmer, too, I learned of the Nuffield Organization's muddled attitude towards its design staff, before *and* after the 1952 merger with Austin which brought the British Motor Corporation into existence. 'We were given very little direction towards the end—or, indeed, in the early days of BMC. Vic Oak [the Nuffield design chief, soon to retire] was a sick man, Issigonis left us to join Alvis . . . It was all very confusing.' In the midst of this confusion, however, Palmer designed the Wolseley 4/44 and its sister, the MG Magnette, plus the Riley Pathfinder and other cars which did not go into production.

While Brocklehurst was with the RAF, Project EX175 was completed around the frame he had designed. It was a good-looking road car, and Thornley asked permission to build it as a replacement for the TD Midget. His request was turned down by Sir Leonard Lord, the autocratic boss of BMC, who had arranged for Donald Healey's Austin A90-engined sports car to be built at Longbridge, Birmingham. But MG urgently needed something to replace the TD, whose export sales were beginning to take a dive. Cowley therefore came up with a TD facelift which appeared at the 1953 London Show as the TF. The result was a further fall in sports car sales, and production dropped by 20 per cent in 1954.

In June of that year, when Roy returned to Abingdon, he found things happening all around him. George Eyston had recommended a new Utah record attempt to boost US sales, and EX175—fitted with wheel spats and cockpit cover—had been tried out in the wind-tunnel. This test proving unsatisfactory, another wide chassis frame had been

Left *Syd Enever and Jimmy Cox check one of the Le Mans MGA engines for power output on the Abingdon testbed, as Project EX 182 gets under way*

Far Left *Cliff Bray uses an assembly jig in the old Experimental Shop to put together one of the chassis frames for the three 1955 Le Mans MGAs*

made up to Roy's design and clothed in a near-replica of the Gardner-MG body. Fitted with an unsupercharged XPEG engine, this new record car, EX179, was shipped out to Utah, where Eyston and Ken Miles drove it at 153.69 mph in August.

As for EX175, it was returned to road-going trim and passed over to Cowley for a full road test. The report, dated 26 May 1954, said that on the by-pass north of Oxford the car had reached a mean maximum of 99.8 mph with hood and sidescreens in place. Its one-way best was a timed 100.5 mph. Carrying two occupants, and with gearchanges made at 6000 rpm, it had accelerated from 0 to 60 mph in 15.8 sec. By T type standards, this was pretty good going.

The situation was further complicated by the fact that Gerry Palmer also designed a new sports two-seater MG, which Brocklehurst remembers with some admiration because it was a monocoque construction—much more up-to-date, really, than Roy's chassis-frame job, and therefore lighter. Palmer once told me that his car weighed only 1350 lb. If his memory is not at fault, this means that his prototype two-seater weighed less than George Phillips' ultra-slim racing TC!

However, the choice was finally made in favour of the Abingdon car. Syd Enever was given the authority to productionize EX175, and provided with additional staff at Abingdon to get things moving. As for Gerry Palmer, he once again left Cowley, this time to work for Vauxhall.

Mechanically the new MG presented few problems because it had been tested both as a road car (EX175) and a successful record-breaker (EX179), and John Thornley estimated that production could begin in April 1955. This persuaded him to enter a three-car team for Le Mans, with the intention of

Tailed by Maglioli's Ferrari, Lockett goes through the Esses at Le Mans. Compared with the situation pictured on page 16, the new MG at least seems to belong in the same century as the Italian car, however much slower it may be!

At Dundrod as at Le Mans, Ted Lund's MGA is about to be overtaken by an Italian sports-racer—this time, Musso's 3-litre Maserati. A split fuel tank put Lund's car out of the TT race after eight laps

revealing the new production car to the public just before race day, 11 June. Unfortunately there was a delay in tooling-up at BMC's Bodies Branch in Coventry, so the Le Mans entry had to be transferred to the prototype category. To the public, the three Le Mans MGs were simply EX182s, the experimental prototypes of a probable new production car. Thornley said he knew they had no chance of winning their class, but hoped that all three would finish the race at about 80 mph average to demonstrate their reliability.

The story of Le Mans 1955 has been told often enough, for the trail of carnage that Levegh's Mercedes blasted through the crowd during the early stages of the race made it the worst disaster in motor racing history. Compared to this, nothing else seemed important. One can only record that two of the three new MGs finished the event, Miles and Lockett in 12th place overall with 248 laps completed (86.17 mph average), and the Lund/Waeffler car 17th, with 230 laps (81.97 mph). The third MG had crashed badly at White House just before its driver, Dick Jacobs, was due to hand over to Joe Flynn. In the confusion of the greater tragedy among the spectators, the gravity of poor

Dick's condition was not at first appreciated, but when it was, Sir Leonard Lord 'pressed every button on his desk' (as John Thornley described it to me). Dick was flown back to England for first-class medical attention, and eventually had the doubtful privilege of reading his own obituary notices.

In September, two of the Le Mans cars plus a replacement for Dick's burned-out MGA were entered for the TT at Dundrod. Originally, two of them were to be dohc cars of different design, but this plan was changed at the last minute, leaving only one dohc MGA to be driven by Ron Flockhart and Johnny Lockett, with pushrod ohv cars for Lund/Stoop and Fairman/Wilson.

By a cruel coincidence there was again a serious pile-up early in the race, causing the deaths of two drivers, followed by another fatal accident later on. This time the only MG to finish was the car shared by Jack Fairman and Peter Wilson, who came 20th overall and fourth in class behind three Porsche 550 Spyders. The Lund/Stoop MGA split its fuel tank and retired after only eight laps; the Flockhart/Lockett dohc job needed several pit stops to change plugs, and retired after 23 laps with what was officially described as 'ignition trouble'.

On 22 September—five days after the Dundrod TT—the new MG sports car was on a stand at the Frankfurt Motor Show, making its first appearance as a vehicle for public sale. So instead of being a new production car of which modified versions were subsequently raced, the MGA was presented to potential buyers as a racing project subsequently modified for production. Although the sequence had been reversed by sheer chance, it was better so. Even the traditionalists who took exception to the shape had to admit that the MGA looked right on the racetracks of the mid-1950s alongside Ferrari, Maserati, Jaguar, Mercedes-Benz and Aston Martin.

Chapter 2
Call it 'M.G. Series MGA'

MG's famous collection of type letters—so casually employed in conversation between sports car enthusiasts that outsiders wonder what the dickens they are talking about—began officially with the allocation of an A prefix to the serial numbers of the 18/80 Mark II, the first MG model whose chassis had been designed specifically *as* an MG chassis throughout. The addition of a second letter or number complicated the issue by producing such combinations as J2, K3, TA, TB and so on, but the basic system was retained for more than a quarter-century.

With Gerry Palmer's Magnette being designated the ZA in 1953 (to be followed by the ZB in 1956), the end of the alphabet had been reached. So the decision was made to go back to the beginning, adding the marque's own initials as an ever-present reminder of the new sports car's identity. Though John Thornley doesn't say so, one of MG's many American dealers may also have suggested that Model A alone would be a pretty ridiculous label to hang on Abingdon's brand-new, ultra-modern sports car.

Officially, then, it was to be the 'M.G. Series MGA', which the motoring magazines rendered variously as M.G. 'A', MG 'A', M.G. A, M.G.A., M.G. Series-M.G.A., or just plain 'A'—this latter defeat-

ing the whole purpose of the car's designation. Abingdon's own abbreviation was MGA, later followed by 'MGA 1600' and 'MGA 1600' (Mark II), both in quotes.

Aft of the heelboard position the original Brocklehurst-designed frame for EX175 and EX179 had been tapered inwards in plan, and the record car was also extensively drilled to lighten it. The EX182 Le Mans cars and the production MGA had frames that were parallel at the rear. Otherwise there were few changes. The front cross-member was closely related to the TF design, as was the suspension, and the rack-and-pinion steering which distinguished Nuffield-based cars at the time was retained. The back axle was a slightly narrower version of that used in the Palmer Magnette, which also provided the brakes: drum all round, two-leading-shoe at the front. In choosing BMC's new B

The EX 179 record car frame, like that of the EX 175 road car, sweeps inwards behind the cockpit (and is also much lightened). Otherwise it closely resembles the EX 182 Le Mans chassis—and that of the production MGA above

type 1489 cc engine (first used, again, in the ZA Magnette), MG finally bade farewell to the aged XPAG unit and its shortlived successor, the XPEG. But there were sound reasons for doing so. The B type engine was available in quantity, it had a better stroke/bore ratio, and was already responding well to tuning for use in the rallying Magnettes. The cylinder head was modified but the Magnette gearbox retained, with an Abingdon-designed remote control assembly.

It is notable that no stylist was involved in the body design. It started with the original Gardner-MG shape, which was the basis of both the Le Mans

Far Left *Percy Standin and Jimmy Cox look self-conscious when photographed at work on a Le Mans engine, lapping the head to the block. Clamped coreplugs are typical of Abingdon practice for competition cars*

Below *The stock 1½-litre engine of BMC's Z-series Magnette saloon as delivered to Abingdon, there to be reworked to power one of the 1955 Le Mans team cars*

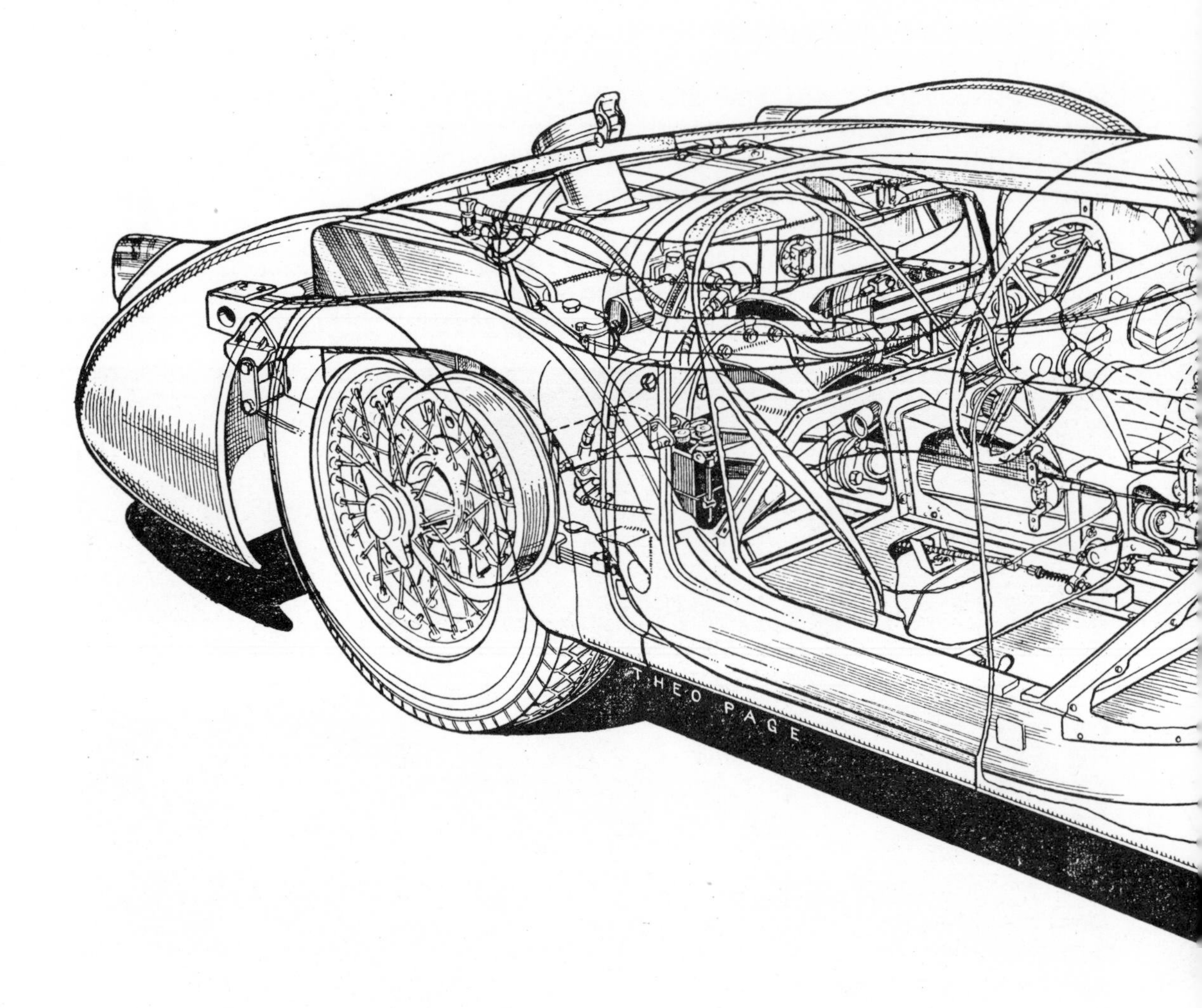

Theo Page's splendid cutaway drawing appeared in Autosport *a week before the 1955 Le Mans race, debut of the three racing MGAs*

AUTOSPORT
COPYRIGHT
LBL 301

Two views of Le Mans chassis number 3 again show the similarity between these and the production MGAs

TD of 1951 and its successor, the roadgoing EX175, plus the EX179 record car. Although the shape was modern the technique employed—going from quarter-scale drawings to fullsize eggbox—was as simple and old-fashioned as could be, until the time came for Bodies Branch to revise the whole thing for production. Most of the early work was done at Abingdon by a growing team of enthusiastic young men—several of them ex-Cowley—working under Syd Enever's direction.

No less remarkable was the fact that the production MGA differed so little from the Le Mans cars. Their bodies were, of course, of aluminium alloy instead of steel, with a panel over the passenger's side of the cockpit, a cowled mirror, and a shallow coaming around the driver, plus a neat plastic racing screen. The passenger's door was fixed for the race, but capable of being opened afterwards, and there were fittings for standard windscreen, sidescreens and top—for these cars, remember, were intended to be used subsequently in the Alpine Rally. There was a full undershield, also removable. The luggage space was completely filled

by a 20-gallon fuel tank—twice the size of the production tank—with quick-release filler protruding through the bootlid. There was a double SU fuel pump mounted very accessibly (would that the production pump had been half as easy to get at!), with large-bore feed to the carburettors. These were 1.75-in., the size later used on the Twin Cam; they had trumpets instead of pancake air-cleaners, and a simple cold-air feed from the left side of the front grille.

The Le Mans cars had no bumpers, of course, and in the front apron there was a double intake for the wide and shallow oil-cooler (quite different from the oil-coolers later marketed as a production option). The oil filter was mounted nearby. Half the front grille was cut away to accommodate a Lucas spotlamp of the type we called 'flamethrowers' in the 1950s, and beside it there was an additional circular intake cut in the body, near the position normally occupied by the heater air intake. For Le Mans, however, the space forward of the bulkhead was mainly taken up by a remote header tank for the radiator. The bonnet had a pair of security

Opposite *Details of an MGA undergoing restoration show the main body section, and the cutaway for the spare wheel in the rear cockpit panel. A removable panel gives access to the batteries*

straps at the front, and an air outlet at the rear end complete with appropriate ducting.

Following normal Abingdon practice for long-distance events, the engine was quite mildly tuned, and output was quoted as a mere 82 bhp on a 9.4:1 compression ratio. At 8 in., the clutch was the same diameter as the later production unit. The brake drums, too, were the same size, but provided with well-shielded cooling holes. The centre-lock wire wheels had alloy rims, and after tests had been made at Le Mans, MG decided on 550 front tyres, 600 rears, with a 3.7:1 final drive and close-ratio gears in the box. The production MGA had the Magnette saloon ratios, with rather a wide gap between second and third, but this was in fact something of an MG tradition—possibly a survival from the days of mud-plugging British trials. The normal final drive for the roadgoing cars was 4.3:1, and the tyre section was 560 front and rear.

Below *EX 179 on the Salt Flats at Utah after topping 170 mph in 1956, using an unblown prototype of the Twin Cam engine. Drivers Lockett and Miles shake hands, with George Eyston in the centre*

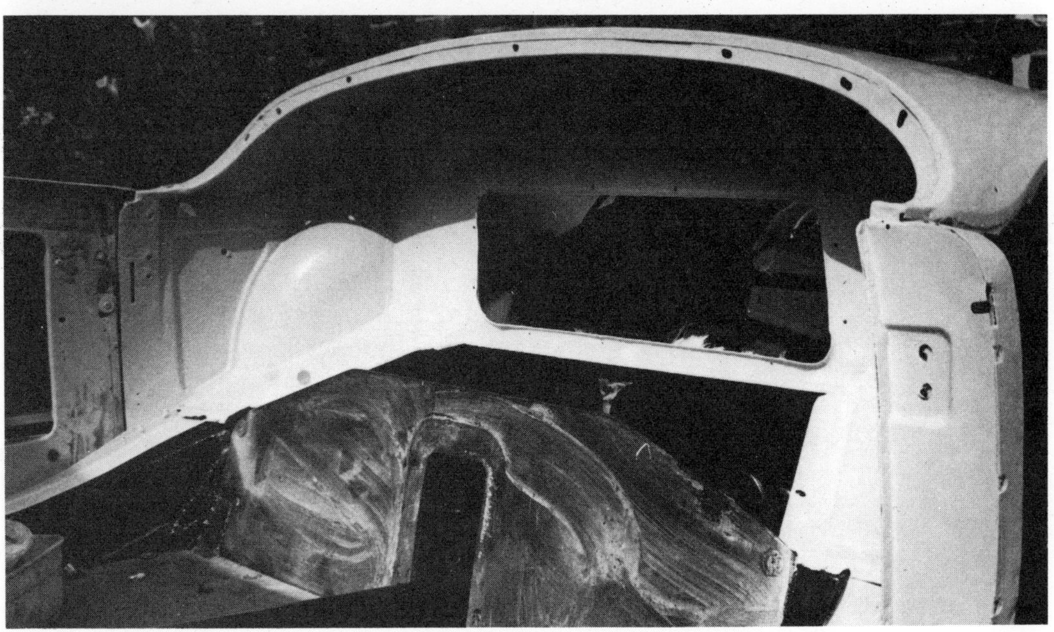

Friendly rivals: Len Ayton of Autocar *and Harold Hastings of* Motor *sample the new car on the MGA's press preview day at Abingdon*

When John Bolster of *Autosport* was able to try one of the steel-bodied production MGAs, he commented: 'Having driven the competition model, EX182, from which this car was derived, I can say that little has been lost and a great deal gained in grooming the machine for production. The excellent roadholding and steering of the prototype are fully retained, and the loss of performance is less than I expected. . . . This is a jolly good little sports car; if you want one, hurry up and get in the queue.' From Bolster, the last man in the world who could be called an MG enthusiast, this was praise indeed.

Autocar, too, had sampled the racer before road-testing the road car (which was in fact the same car that Bolster was later to drive), and made almost the same comment: 'There are naturally some differences . . . but the roadholding, braking and

The lines of the tail were clean and uncluttered, but. . .

. . .inside, the spare wheel took up most of the trunk. However, no T-type had this much luggage space

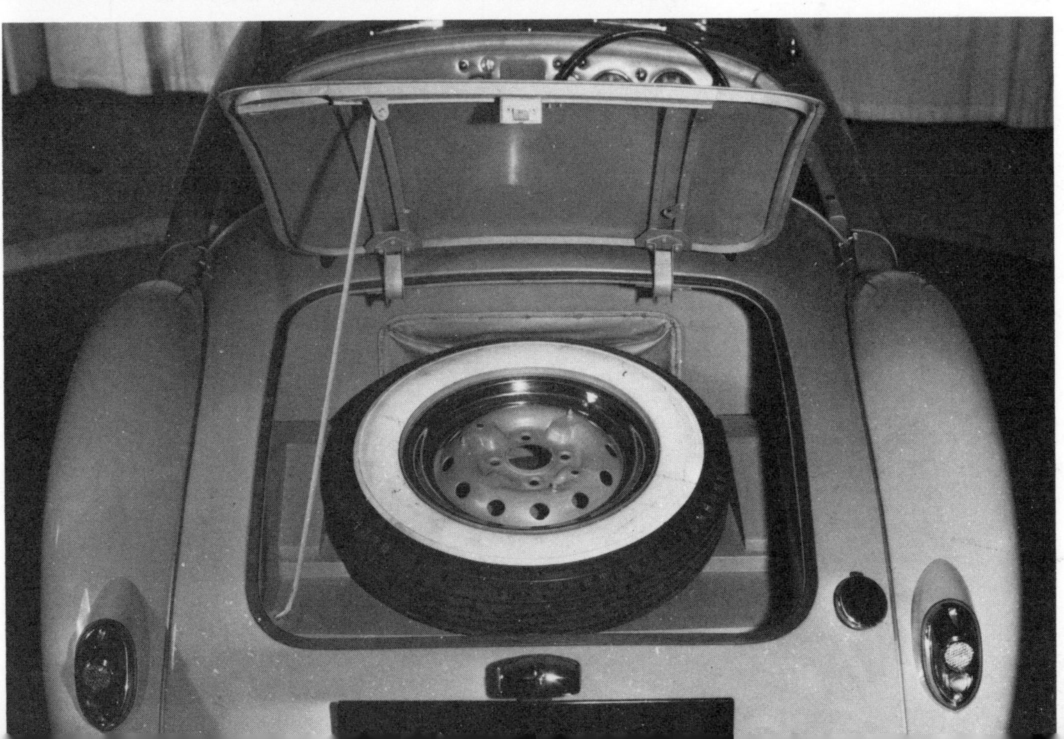

Above *This MGA 1500 has the old-style, non-opening sidescreens with spring-loaded signalling flap at the bottom*

Left *By T-type standards, the MGA had a roomy cockpit. The windscreen struts made useful handholds for passengers*

American journalist John Bentley tries an early MGA on country roads near the Abingdon works

steering are unaffected, and in these respects the MGA recalls very intimately the Le Mans car. The brand-new M.G. sports two-seater confounds the critics who say that racing teaches no useful lessons.'

Motor, perhaps surprisingly, made no mention of the MGA's racing debut, but also made no bones about its opinion of the car. 'The newest M.G. must be summed up as enthusiastically as it was everywhere received. That the modern style is generally approved there can be no doubt, but far more important is the introduction of a small car with a degree of roadworthiness high by any standards. The famous slogan of the factory has indeed never been better applied.'

And on the other side of the Atlantic *Road & Track*, in a report headlined 'A Classic Sports Car Goes Modern', said: 'Now the break with tradition is complete. The car is indeed "all new", and we feel that early enthusiasm for its appearance can now be augmented by the knowledge of its very surprising performance. We also feel it is not stretching a point to say that anybody who likes anything about

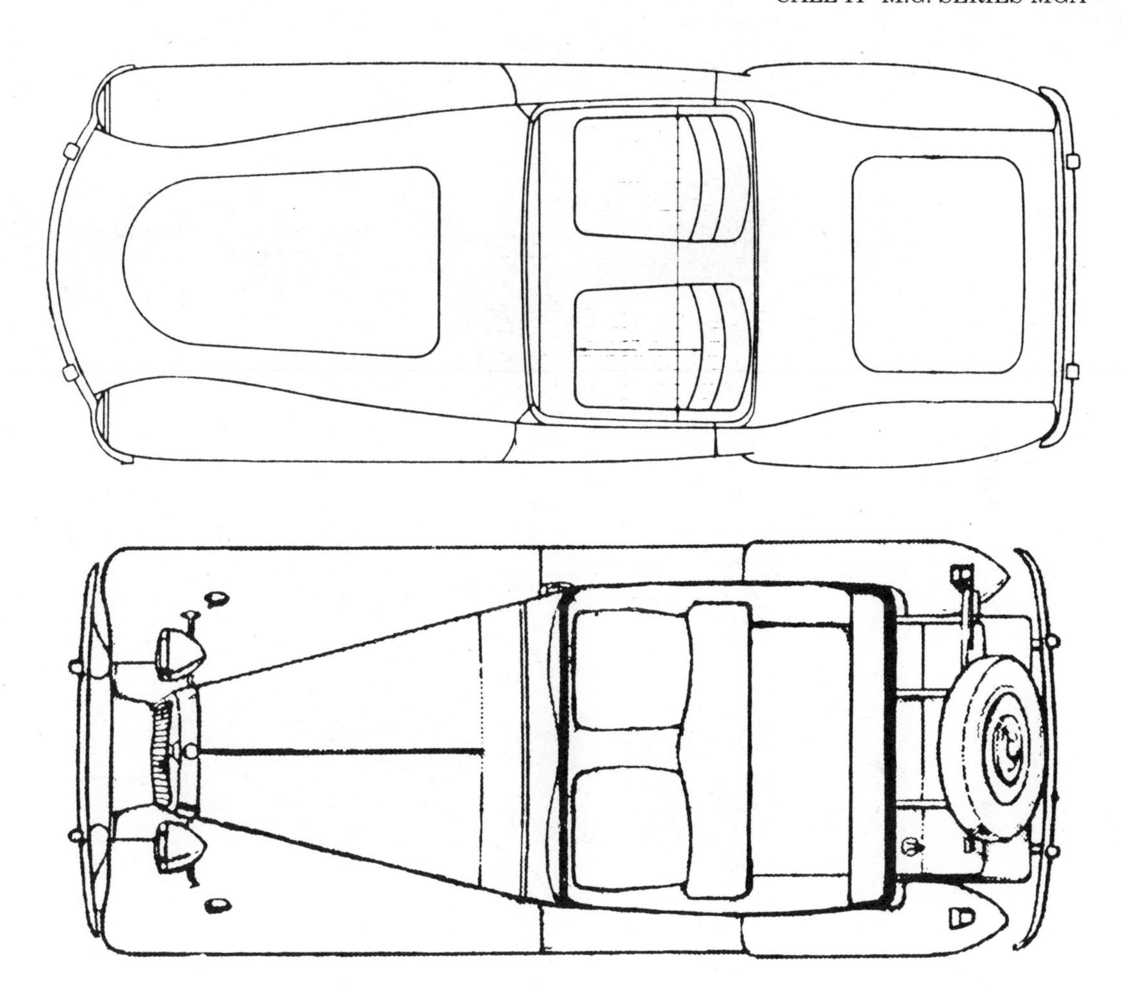

MGA 1500		TD Midget
94″	Wheelbase	94″
47.5″	Track (F)	47.38″
48.75″	Track (R)	50″
156″	Length	145″
58″	Width	58.63″
50″	Height	53″
37″	Headroom	35″
45″	Interior width	45″
29″	Seatfront to toeboard (mean)	23″
16″	Seatback to wheel rim (mean)	12″
6″	Wheel rim to seat cushion	5.5″
39″ × 30″ × 14″	Luggage space (approx)	36″ × 21″ × 14.5″
1980 lb	Kerb weight	2016 lb

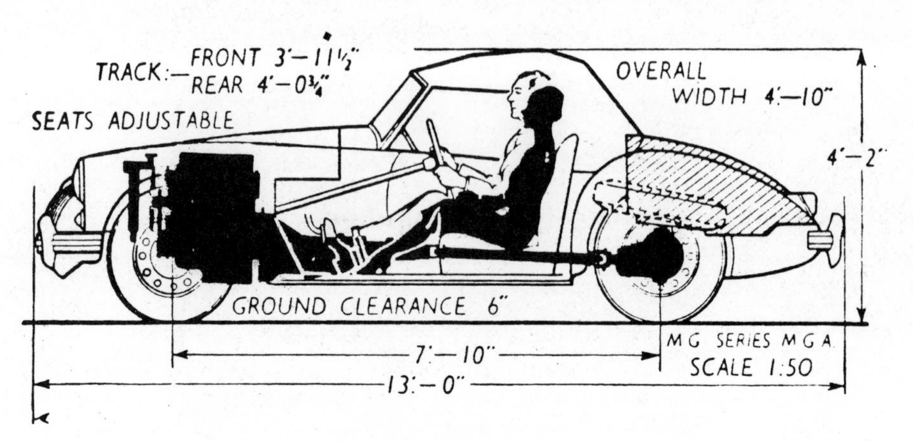

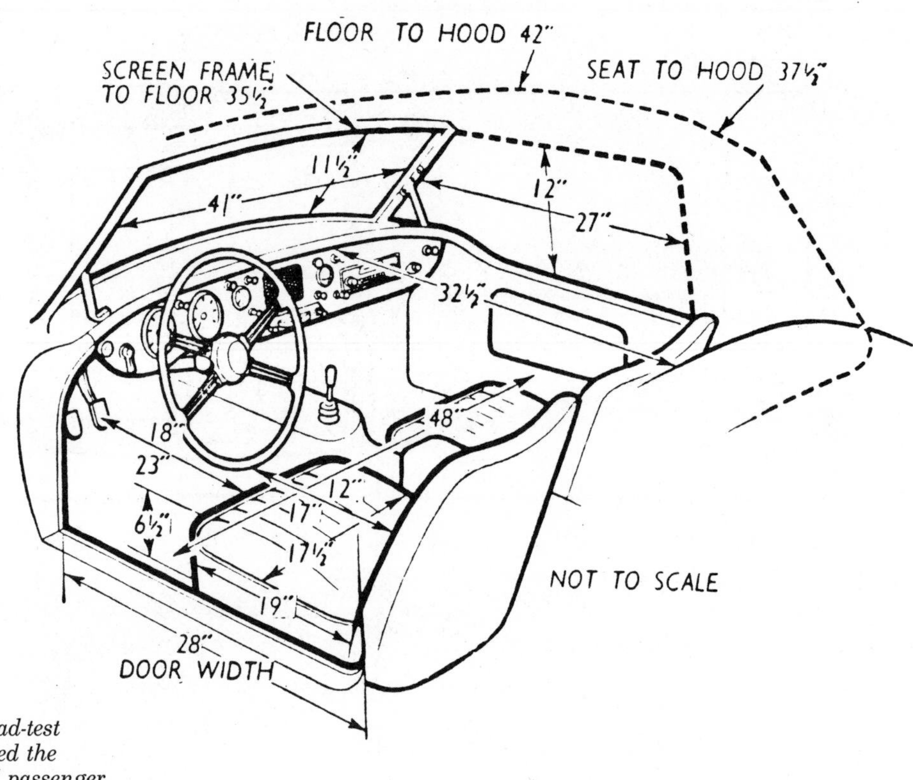

Contemporary road-test reports emphasized the MGA's improved passenger and luggage space compared to the TD; no full-scale road test of the TF was published in British magazines

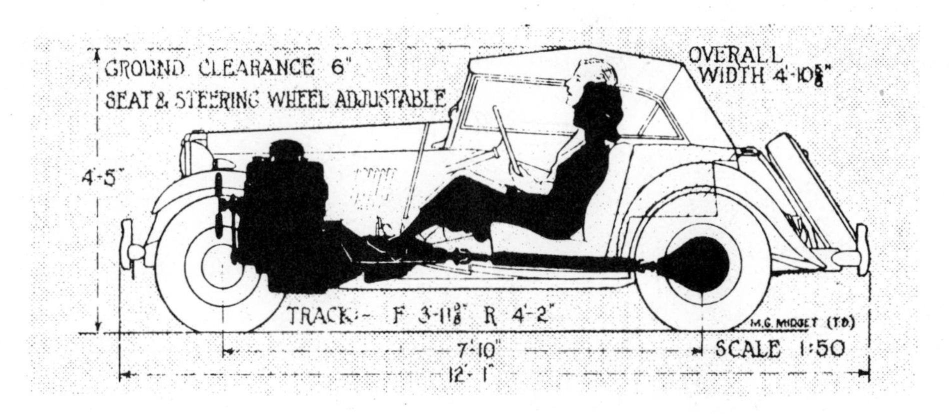
GROUND CLEARANCE 6"
SEAT & STEERING WHEEL ADJUSTABLE
OVERALL WIDTH 4'-10⅝"
4'-5"
TRACK:- F 3'-11⅞" R 4'-2"
M.G. MIDGET (T.D)
7'-10"
SCALE 1:50
12'-1"

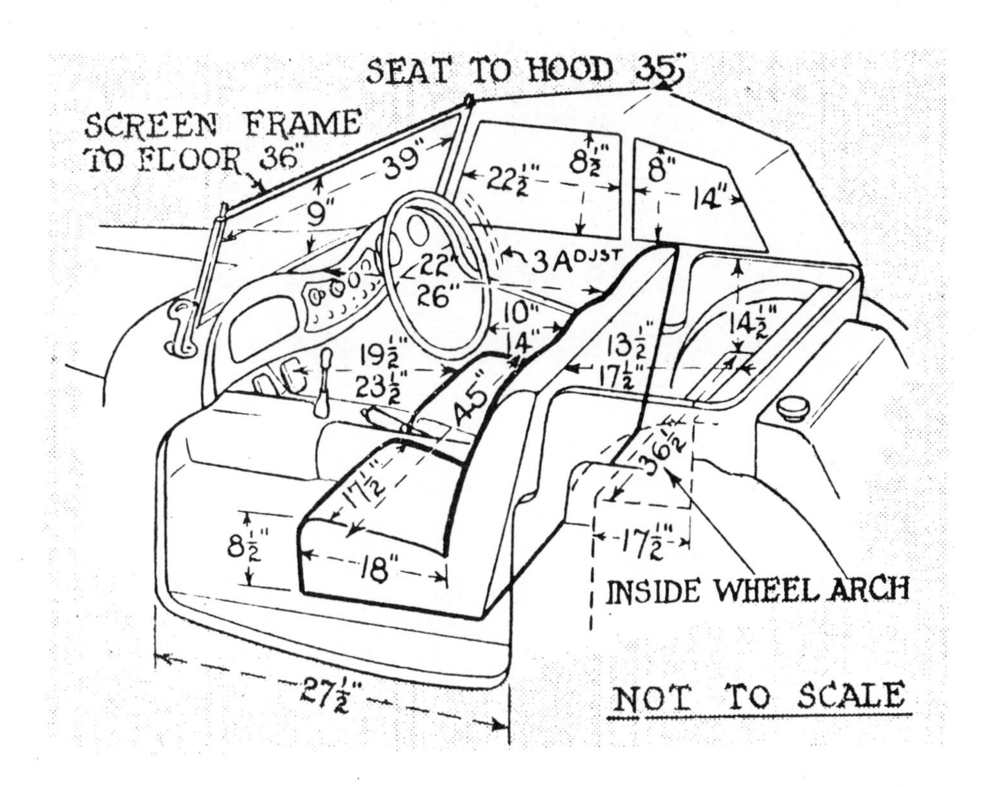
SEAT TO HOOD 35"
SCREEN FRAME TO FLOOR 36"
39"
9"
22½"
8½"
8"
14"
3 ADJST
22"
26"
10"
14"
19½"
23½"
13½"
17½"
14½"
45"
17½"
36½"
8½"
18"
17½"
INSIDE WHEEL ARCH
27½"
NOT TO SCALE

Two Silverstone pictures reveal the difference in driving position. J. D. Hall is head-and-shoulders above the aero screen of his TF1500. Chris Tooley, not at all undersized, sits snugly in the ex-works MGA he raced for several seasons

a sports car will be more than pleased with the new MG. . . . If you look over the MG "A" with a critical eye, drive it and note the price tag—you will probably ask the same question we do: How are they going to supply enough cars to meet the demand?'

The UK price tag of an MGA, excluding tax because the government changed it from time to time, was £595. This was the same price as Peter Morgan's TR-engined Plus Four, and £55 less than the Triumph TR3. Only three sports cars on the British market cost less: the stark Ford-engined Dellow trials car (£448), the new Ford-engined Morgan 4/4 (£450) and the regrettable Singer Roadster (£510), which was fast approaching its demise. An Austin-Healey 100 cost £750, an HRG was listed at £895, but as the same figure would buy a 2.4-litre Jaguar, the HRG was also near to extinction. The Jaguar XK140 was rated excellent value for money at a basic £1140—but this was, after all, nearly twice the price of the new MG.

To set the scene for the MGA's performance figures, a check-up shows that of 30 cars tested in 1955/56 by *Motor* and 33 by *Autocar*, only half-a-dozen bettered 19 sec for the standing quarter-mile. In order of price they were the Triumph TR3 (basic price £735 with hardtop and overdrive); Jaguar XK140 (£1140); Jensen 541 (£1435); Ford Thunderbird (£1690); Packard Clipper (£2475); and Rolls-

MGAs in Canada (above), *Australia* (above right) *and Sweden* (below right) *emphasize the new model's world-wide appeal*

Royce Silver Cloud (£3385). A further half-dozen (Austin A105, Jaguar 2.4, Jaguar Mark VII, Porsche 1600, AC Aceca and Bentley Series S) broke the 20-second barrier, their prices ranging from £739 to £3295. Over the same period, *Motor* found only five cars that would achieve a genuine 100-plus mean maximum, but *Autocar* cast their net wider to bring in a further 11 examples. Taking all 16 cars, the prices ranged from the £735 of the hardtop TR3 to the Rolls-Royce Silver Cloud's then dizzy price tag of £3385.

As for the MGA, it neither achieved 100 mph nor covered the standing quarter-mile in less than 19 sec, but it came close enough to both to impress its testers considerably. When they assessed the car's other good qualities against the background of its price, they had no hesitation in expressing their approval.

34
HGG 268

35
35
16
16

The figures recorded were surprisingly close. *Autocar* did the standing quarter in 20.2 sec, and their other acceleration times ranged from 4.9 sec to 30 mph, through 15.6 sec to 60 mph, to 50.1 sec to 90 mph. With a different car, *Motor*'s figures were 20.4 sec, 4.9 (again), 16.0 and 44.6 sec. *Autosport*, driving the same car as *Autocar* but about a month later, returned 20 sec dead, 4.8 sec to 30 mph and 15.0 sec to 60, but quoted no figure to 90 mph. Nor did *Road & Track*, whose standing quarter occupied 19.6 sec with 4.6 sec to 30 mph and 14.5 to 60 mph. From rest to 80 mph the four magazines clocked respectively 32.1, 30.0, 31.2 and 30.4 sec. Turning to maximum speed, the same four reported it as 98.0, 97.8, 96.7 and 95.1 mph, referring in each case to a timed two-way average. The best one-way speed was *Autocar*'s 99.0, but to achieve this they fitted a half tonneau cover and a small aero screen instead of the standard full-width windscreen.

MGAs in Southern Rhodesia (far left), *Switzerland* (left) *and Southern Ireland* (below) *continue the theme of international appreciation*

1057 224

Road & Track referred back to an earlier test of the TF 1500 to make an interesting comparison, demonstrating the effect of the new body shape. Up to 30 mph, the improvement in acceleration was 4.1 per cent; at 50 mph the improvement was 7.3 per cent, and at 70 mph it had risen to 19.4 per cent. Maximum speed was up by 10 mph, and fuel consumption reduced by more than 20 per cent. To spell out loud and clear the value of the new shape, *R & T* reported that at 60 mph the total drag of the TF was 119 lb, compared to just 94 lb for the MGA. The reduction in wind and rolling resistance therefore amounted to just over 21 per cent.

Naturally, all the testers found something to criticize in the MGA. All had some doubts about the seats, finding them lacking in support for the thighs, or too upright, or badly shaped for the lumbar region. One reckoned the steering wheel was too close to the chest; two felt it was too close to the legs. Luggage space was rated anything from moderate to inadequate, *Autocar* expressed surprise at the old-fashioned screw-type jack, and *Motor* noted the inaccessibility of the batteries. One said the top vibrated over 70 mph, another thought it almost impossible to raise or lower single-handed, but a third said the weather equipment was perfection. Remembering that the headlamp wattage was a mere 42/36, one marvels that only Bolster said the lights were barely adequate for fast night driving. Even more surprisingly, only *Autocar* recorded the infuriating position of the dipswitch, which called for a left foot of massive proportions to operate it conveniently.

Autocar noted, too, how first gear sometimes baulked engagement in the familiar BMC fashion, and the unduly strong spring that guarded reverse gear. *Motor* rated second gear a little too low, and on their car had some trouble with a jerky throttle cable. The engine, they said, was noisy by touring-

Far Left *An American MGA owner enjoys his British sports car in a muddy, British-style autocross near St Louis*

The MGA seems equally at home in an Austrian hillclimb (right) *or transporting local beauty queens to the judging arena in Tasmania* (below)

car standards, and sometimes inclined to run-on after a fast drive. *Road & Track* remarked mildly that the MGA, with its wide sills and low seat, was not too easy to get into, but nobody said a word about the absence of exterior handles for the doors or boot-lid, or the difficulty of locating the door pull-cables when top and screens were in place. They didn't even ask where valuables could be stowed under lock and key; petty thieving must then have been unusual instead of inevitable, as it is today.

Road & Track quickly summed up the special quality of the MGA's road behaviour: 'As always, the MG is still the perfect car for the tyro enthusiast. It handles faultlessly and can be cornered and drifted by a beginner almost immediately. Compared to a car with independent rear suspension, the MG rear end drifts out rather more easily than expected, but there is neither understeer nor oversteer.'

Motor, on the same topic, went into considerable

When the wings are removed, the wide ratio of track to overall height becomes obvious. The MGA stands foursquare on the ground as if to spell out its inherent stability

detail to try and convey this quality, and did it so well that their comments deserve to be quoted in full. This is how it was described:

'To drive the M.G.A. on a winding open road is sheer enthusiast's delight. Rack and pinion steering and small cars have always gone well together, and the lightness of the steering with a small, four-spoked wheel is matched by a quickness and precision which might not be expected from the lock-to-lock figure (for a very compact lock) of $2\frac{3}{4}$ turns. In this case the secret lies in an admirable example of useful and controllable oversteer. In point of fact an improvement in handling was found possible by inflating the tyres from the recommended fast-driving pressures of 18 lb. front and 23 lb. for the rear wheels to approximately 26 lb. on all four. The effect of the oversteer then was merely that the driver, rather like a pilot in some types of aircraft, steered into a turn and then virtually centralized the wheel to keep the car on its course.

'Quite apart from steering characteristics, the cornering power of the car is extremely good, holding it down in a manner to give the driver complete confidence, and seemingly almost indifferent to the type of road surface. As is often the case, a wet road gives an earlier indication of the car's behaviour when pressed to the limit on a corner, sliding of the rear wheels beginning quite gradually and being easily transformed into a controlled drift.'

Though the driver of today may wonder how a 16.5 in. steering wheel can possibly be described as *small*, no-one who has ever driven an MGA fast on a winding road, steering it almost entirely with the right foot instead of two hands, will fail to recognize from that passage that *Motor* got it right. The man who wrote those words very clearly and obviously knew what the MGA was all about, and had a quietly splendid time finding it out.

Chapter 3
Coupé Twin Cam and 1600

During 1956, MG brought out an extremely well-made hardtop for the MGA, and thick plastic sliding sidescreens instead of the flimsy devices with spring-loaded signalling flap which were used on the early open cars. This set-up was the norm in international rallies. Works drivers had no time to fool about with folding tops, and recognized long before ordinary mortals did that for those who had to maintain high average speeds with minimal fatigue, open sports cars had had their day. They wanted a vehicle that was free from draughts and rattles, reasonably leakproof in the wet, and offering some assurance that a precious map or roadbook would not go flying over a mountainside to be lost for ever, taking with it the chance of a possible class-win. Perhaps to satisfy some obscure requirement of the *Fédération Internationale de l'Automobile* Appendix J regulations, the hardtop MGA was even listed as a separate model, separately advertized, and with its own separate brochure. Oddly enough, the hardtop was always black although the car could then be had in black, red, green, blue or white.

A convenient side-effect of the hardtop was that its smooth and non-vibrating shape added several mph to the MGA's maximum speed, with little effect on acceleration because the weight was not greatly increased. There remained the problem that valuables could not be effectively locked away, and in summertime the hardtop could make the car stuffy—a disadvantage that the sliding screens did little to alleviate, as they opened only at the rear. For the 1956 London Show, then, Abingdon announced a fixed-head coupé in addition to the open two-seater. Its lines reproduced almost exactly the shape of the hardtop model, but the opportunity was taken to incorporate quite a useful wraparound and additional height in the windscreen, with a noticeable gain in visibility. The doors featured exterior handles, locks, winding windows and hinged quarter-flaps for ventilation. The instrument panel was Vynide-covered and the interior of the car tidied-up in detail.

Unavoidably, the weight went up by about 160 lb, but as the MGA engine had meanwhile been revised to provide an extra 4 bhp over the 68 bhp of the earliest open cars, John Bolster's test for *Autosport* recorded marginally improved acceleration, with a 0 to 60 mph time of 14.2 sec and 19.2 sec for the standing quarter; the open two-seater, if retested with the same engine, would of course have shown even better figures for acceleration, but would not have matched his 102.27 mph maximum speed with the coupé.

In theory the fixed-head coupé was meant to serve as a convenient little Grand Touring machine for those who wanted a reasonable turn of performance, were not enamoured of the folding-top sports car, and would, it was thought, enjoy a measure of refinement—a touch of class— for £100-odd more than the normal MGA price. Unfortunately the luggage space was too restricted for the coupé to satisfy this market effectively; also the fixed roof tended to magnify engine noise, and heat radiating from the gearbox could make the car uncomfortably hot at times. Although the interior

Above *With a certain naïve charm, the original 'MG Series MGA' brochure, claimed that MG's latest model would 'meet the challenge of* tomorrow *on road and track'*

Left *Brian Sterling drives his 1500 roadster in a parade at Brands Hatch, 1975. Teal Blue may not be 'correct' for an MGA 1500—but it's a very attractive colour!*

Right *A close look at the Twin Cam brochure shows that no Twin Cam was available to the photographer; he used a stock 1500 and retouched the wheels, not too convincingly!*

Below *Nigel Smith's 1958 Twin Cam has been repainted, but he has resisted the temptation to change the original interior trim*

Left *The brochures for the 1600 and 1600 Mark II differed little. The first showed the wrong sidelights, tinted to appear correct for the UK (but not the USA). The second got them almost right for a US-market car, and of course featured the pre-accidented front grille of the Mark II*

Below *Fred Downs of Yeovil has done an extensive restoration on his MGA 1600 roadster*

YGO 180

Left *Roy Coomber's 1959 Twin Cam coupé, bought almost 20 years ago for £475, is a frequent concours award winner, destined for permanent display at Beaulieu when the owner gives up driving*

Above *Piers Hubbard, for many years MGCC honorary treasurer, is another award-winner with this well-known 1600 Mark II roadster*

Overleaf *Fred Scatley's shot of MGAs taking Paddock Bend, Brand's Hatch, in 1980 shows how the club-racing MGA looks nowadays when given the treatment. The yellow car is Roy McCarthy's very successful machine*

1817 PX

Right *By contrast to the Modified cars, R. T. Marsh's Twin Cam roadster and John Wright's 1622 cc coupé, seen here at Silverstone's Woodcote Corner in 1982, seem much less removed from stock MGAs—however much modified in detail*

Below *MG Car Club members get together at Beaulieu, 1982, for their annual rally in the grounds of the National Motor Museum. Red is obviously the favourite MGA colour nowadays*

was partially redesigned in mid-1959 to provide more space behind the seats, it was still very cramped by GT standards. Rather surprisingly, the MGA coupé proved more useful—usually on a Twin Cam chassis, and with either the Twin Cam or a well-tuned 1600 engine—as a long-distance racing and rally car. But that belongs in the next chapter.

As for the Twin Cam, it had been the subject of rumour and speculation for almost three years by the time it was finally revealed in mid-July 1958. At a basic price of £854, this was only about £180 more than the pushrod MGA 1500 at that time, and it is a great pity that the Twin Cam is now remembered more for its vices than its virtues. MG were, of necessity, old hands at extracting remarkable power outputs from unremarkable engines, but the way the MGA unit's maximum power had been increased by 50 per cent was little short of miraculous—especially as it had been done, as always, on a very limited budget. Few production engines of a quarter-century ago would respond to a touch of the throttle like the Twin Cam, which (as its critics tend to overlook when they dismiss it as unduly temperamental) produced only 5 bhp less than a supercharged eight cylinder 1.5-litre Bugatti, and had a top speed some 5 mph higher than that of the 1926 Grand Prix car. Indeed, the way the tachometer needle flashed around the dial, to the accompaniment of a blast of sound from the exhaust, was highly reminiscent of a supercharged machine.

But a comparison with a car from the distant past—even one as famous as the Type 39—is perhaps fairly meaningless. Instead, we can make use of published performance figures to 'organize' a drag contest that probably never happened, just to see what the result would be.

Let us park an MGA Twin Cam side-by-side with a Jaguar XK120 on an empty road. Both are

The MGA raodster with hardtop and sliding screens was listed as a separate model early in 1956, and closely resembles the fixed-head coupé announced later that year. Closer inspection reveals the exterior handles on the doors, glass windows with ventilators, and wider and higher screen

production two-seater sports cars. The MG weighs about 26 per cent less than the Jaguar, but the Jag is powered by a 3442 cc six-cylinder engine—well over twice the capacity of the MG's 1588 cc four-cylinder. Now stand back, drop an imaginary starting flag, and see what happens.

Up to 30 mph the MG will be almost a second ahead, and, as you might expect because of its lighter weight, it is still leading at 40. At 50 mph, the MG is momentarily checked by a change into third gear while the Jaguar is still accelerating hard in second, but at 60 mph it's the Jaguar's turn to change up. We notice with some surprise that at this stage the MG is still almost half-a-second ahead. Now that both cars are in third gear, the Jaguar driver (beginning to go a little pink in the face, perhaps ?) is still unable to catch the MG at 70. He is

even more embarrassed to find the Abingdon product *still* holding him off at 80 mph. But then, as the MG man changes into top while the Jaguar has another 7 mph to go in third gear, the big six at last gets past the four-cylinder car to open out a 1.1-second gap between them at 90. After 40.3 sec, the MG is travelling at exactly 100 mph, whereas the Jaguar is getting close to 110.

Finally, with both cars travelling flat-out, the Jaguar is just about touching the 120 mph which gave the car its type number. The MG (for which some folk claim the same top speed) is dropping back, some 3 or 4 mph slower at the top end. If, however, conditions change and repeated brake applications are called for because of corners or slower cars in the way, the Jaguar man is very soon in trouble with his notoriously inadequate drum

The 1600 version of the coupé had a narrower rear shelf and the spare wheel was confined to the trunk, allowing more stowage space behind the seats

brakes. The MG driver smiles with quiet satisfaction, unconcerned by thoughts of overheating and sudden lining fade as he uses his all-round disc brakes to the full.

Substitute an Aston Martin DB2 (2580 cc, six cylinders, dohc) for the Jaguar, and the result will be quite similar. The Aston will remain behind the MG for almost a quarter of a mile, then pull ahead to reach 100 mph some 5 sec before its rival—but with the interesting difference that in *this* imaginary contest the Aston Martin runs out of steam at 110 mph, so the MG edges past it again to draw gradually ahead, with just sufficient advantage in top speed to keep it there. And the Aston, like the Jaguar, has drum brakes. . . .

Yet another way of describing Twin Cam acceleration is, quite simply, that an incompetent driver could wreck the engine with his right foot; the orange (go easy, there!) sector of the tachometer was from 6500 to 7000, and the needle reached it awfully quickly. After that you were in the red—in every sense. The very high compression ratio called for 100-octane fuel at a time when it was by no means generally available—especially overseas, where 83 per cent of all Twin Cams were sold. To set the ignition timing and mixture strength called for meticulous care and an intimate knowledge of the textbook settings—and these, too, were not easy to find in some parts of the world, where service operators were more accustomed to big, soft, low-output engines that could stand any amount of abuse.

Early in 1962, Jaguar personality Ian Appleyard drove a fixed-head Mark II coupé when taking his Institute of Advanced Motorists test with George Eyles

Even some of the more experienced drivers were caught out by the ready-revving characteristics of the Twin Cam. A car supplied to one of Britain's most famous monthly magazines for road-test came back with bent valves, proving that it had been allowed to stray well into the red zone. Roy Brocklehurst recalls an occasion when he and Alec Hounslow took one of the Development Dept cars onto the Motor Industry Research Association's banked track for extended testing. 'There was a funny noise, so we opened the bonnet and unscrewed the sparking-plugs. I'll never forget it: the sun was shining on the top end of the con rod—we could see it glinting through the plughole. The piston crown wasn't there any more. . . .'

The Twin Cam's centrelock, peg-drive steel wheels (with slightly larger-section tyres) were an immediate recognition feature, and a source of delight to all who admired their functional efficiency. Behind them, the Dunlop disc brakes were barely visible. Looking more closely at the car, one noticed that besides the 'Twin Cam' flashes on the bodywork, there were new and better seats and the instrument panel was Vynide-covered, as on the fixed-head coupé version of the 1500. Lifting the

Right *With massive alloy cylinder head, sump, timing chest and camshaft covers, the Twin Cam engine bears little resemblance to the original BMC unit on page 37*

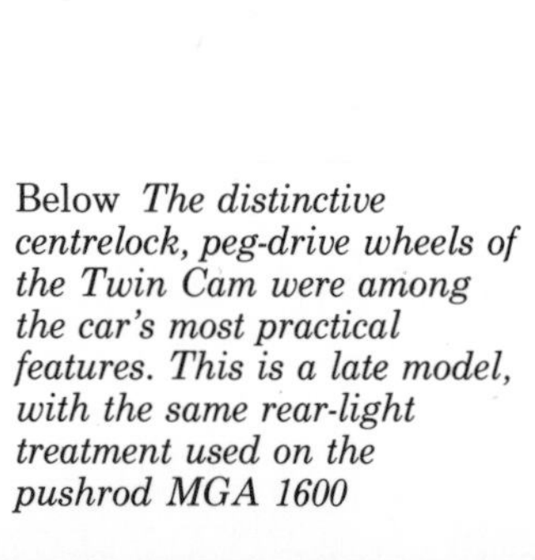

Below *The distinctive centrelock, peg-drive wheels of the Twin Cam were among the car's most practical features. This is a late model, with the same rear-light treatment used on the pushrod MGA 1600*

bonnet revealed that the (larger) carburettors were on the right of the engine instead of the left, so the heater was turned around and its inlet hose ran along the left side, not the right. The big alloy cylinder head with its gleaming camshaft covers took up a lot of room. So did the remote header tank at the left. Accessibility was definitely not one of the virtues of the Twin Cam—too many of the auxiliaries were lost from view further down.

Motor commented that the engine was noisy when the throttle was opened wide, and their test car dropped below the 20 mpg mark when it was hustled somewhat. There were no complaints of heavy oil consumption, although this, too, could be a Twin Cam habit; it probably helped that the car tested had the optional oil-cooler installed. Surprisingly, the front dampers gave enough trouble to be rated virtually useless after 1500 miles, causing front-end vibration and scuttle shake.

As in reporting on the MGA 1500, however, *Motor*'s tester put his finger on the thing that mattered most: 'Stated thus baldly, the plain facts of roadholding behaviour may not convey to a reader unfamiliar with the M.G.A its most endearing characteristics: that of being fun to drive. This quality as a whole is hard to pin down, yet instantly recognizable by anyone coming fresh to the car, and is probably owed to the obvious but not universal circumstance of a set of controls which all work perfectly.'

MGA production reached its first peak of 20,571 cars in 1957, dropped back slightly in 1958, and with the help of the Twin Cam went on to its highest level—23,319 cars built—in 1959. On 31 July that year the MGA 1500 was replaced by the 1600, which had two main new features compared to its predecessor: the engine had been opened out to Twin Cam capacity, and disc brakes had been fitted at the front (together with a change in linings for the rear

Phil Hill tries the author's Twin Cam in 1960, the year after driving the Twin Cam-engined EX 181 record car, and the year before becoming the first American to win the World Championship of Grand Prix drivers

Though discontinued, the Twin Cam remained a popular choice for sports car racing and is still raced today (see colour section)

Bob Olthoff drives his first race in England, 1960. A South African who worked at Abingdon for a time, he was one of the fastest Twin Cam operators

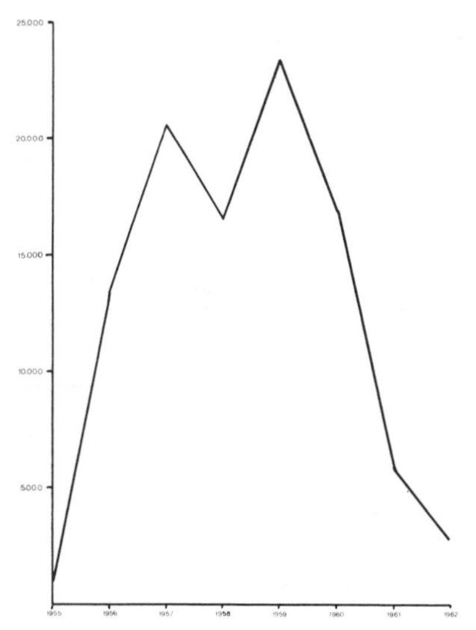

Initial success of the MGA 1500 was spectacular, soaring in 1957 to more than double MG's previous record for one year's production. After a slight fallback in 1958 it was seemingly helped by the Twin Cam (from late 1958) and 1600 Mark I (mid-1959) to a still higher total. American sales of most British sports cars fell sharply towards the end of that year; the MGA was no exception

brakes). Minor changes included improvements to the folding top, standardizing the sliding-type sidescreens, and regrouping the pedals to improve the dipswitch position. Larger sidelights were fitted at the front, their lenses varying according to local regulations; in Britain the lower section was clear and the upper (flasher) portion was tinted amber. The tail-lights, too, were changed, with a new plinth on which separate flashers were mounted—amber for the UK market, red overseas. New colours—of which the strangest, perhaps, was called Alamo Beige to please Texans and bewilder everyone else— were listed for the bodywork. The price of the car was unchanged.

The new brakes made good sense: experience had shown that all-round discs (as on the Twin Cam) demanded higher pedal pressures than drum brakes at low speed, and of course made it difficult to provide an efficient handbrake. Front discs and rear drums (by Lockheed, not Dunlop) were an excellent compromise where high-speed performance was not the primary consideration. In the early life of the 1600 they did, however, suffer from squeal and rapid wear, as a result of which they were fitted with shields to keep dust and grit out of the calipers.

Autocar and *Motor* both approved of the brakes when testing the 1600, and expressed even louder approval of the MGA's performance with its larger engine (albeit at the cost of inferior mpg). The extra 7.5 bhp of power output was hardly world-shaking, but it was accompanied by a substantial improvement in torque which worked wonders for the acceleration, especially in top gear, making it therefore more flexible than before. From a standstill to 30 mph occupied 4.3 sec for *Motor*, 4.6 sec for *Autocar*. The time to 60 mph achieved by *Motor* (13.3 sec) was 2.7 sec better than with the 1500, though *Autocar*'s 14.2 sec was only 1.4 sec better than their previous figure. *Motor*'s car reached 80 mph in 25.1 sec (a 4.9-second improvement), and *Autocar*'s 26.6 sec was 5.5 sec quicker than before. The two weekly magazines recorded 19.8 and 19.3 sec respectively for the standing-start quarter-mile. *Motor* managed a two-way 96.1 mph and a one-way 100 mph with their road-test MGA 1600, SM0 907. *Autocar* did rather better with theirs, SM0 908, quoting a mean 100.9 mph and a 101.4 mph best speed.

Getting away from mere figures, the MGA 1600 was revealed as a faster and more flexible car than the 1500, with a significant improvement in braking power that more than matched its increased performance, and no loss of previous good features. Which was the way Abingdon liked to do things.

Nevertheless, 1959/60 brought a considerable recession in US sports car sales which hit the British exporters equally hard—MG, Morgan, Jaguar and Triumph all suffered at the same time. As the MGA's replacement was not yet ready for production, there was not much that Abingdon could do about the situation. Experiments in totally revamping the MGA body shape with help from Frua of Italy had proved abortive, merely confirming that no significant change could be made without abandoning the MGA chassis altogether. And that, inevitably, was going to take a while.

Meanwhile, reports from America in particular indicated that the service history of the Twin Cam was posing problems. Never mind whether the fault lay with the factory, the dealer's service department, or the owners of the cars—it was felt that Twin Cam troubles were having a damaging effect on the sale of pushrod MGAs. In retrospect, this view may have been unduly alarmist, since we know that sales of *all* British sports cars were down at this time. However, immediately after the 1960 Sebring race it was agreed that the Twin Cam should be discontinued. So quickly was the decision implemented that Abingdon had a fairly substantial stock of Twin Cam components in hand. Most were used up over the course of the next couple of years by building the cars with pushrod-ohv engines instead, calling them the MGA 1600 De Luxe because they had the Twin Cam's better seats, covered dash, all-round disc brakes and special wheels. But one MG collector, who had not yet bought himself a Twin Cam, persuaded John Thornley to make him one after production had officially ended.

In April 1961 came the MGA 1600 Mark II, destined to remain in production for little more than a year, plugging the gap until the new MGB was ready for the market. The unfortunate Mark II—apart from having one of the clumsiest labels ever hung on a car—was one of the most under-appreciated models of all times. Almost everybody dismissed it as a minor facelift of the earlier MGA 1600, and almost everybody was wrong. It was in fact a much better car in many respects, most of which were overlooked in the hasty and inaccurate assumption that the existing engine had simply been bored out a little to make it 1622 cc.

What MG had actually done was to redesign the

899 CFC

When first announced in July 1959, the MGA 1600 used a cheaper version of the sliding sidescreens first seen on the catalogued 'MGA hardtop'

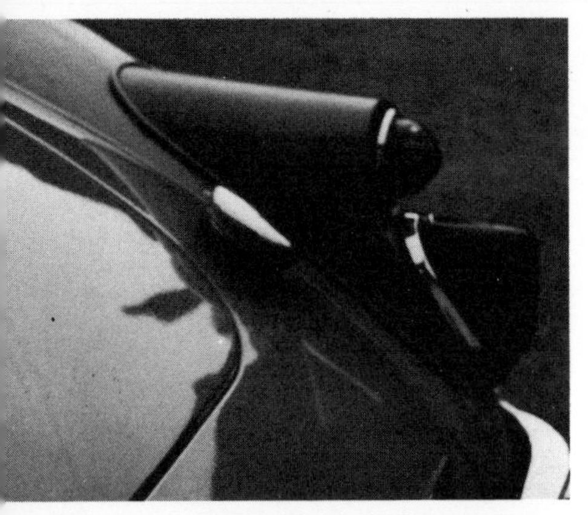

engine all the way through. The new crankshaft had wider, sturdier webs (achieved by reducing the main-bearing width), and the whole engine block was changed. There were new pistons and connecting rods, and a redesigned flywheel which was lighter than before. The gearbox casing was ribbed for greater rigidity. Even the ignition distributor was new. The cylinder head was completely revamped: the combustion chambers had been reshaped and the valves enlarged by 0.062 in., with stronger outer springs. The effect was to raise the peak power output (gross) by 12 per cent to 93 bhp at 5500 rpm—which was slightly lower down the curve than before. This was with a compression ratio of 8.9:1, now standardized because better fuel was more readily available by this time.

It came, alas, too late to save the Twin Cam—most of whose problems, it was now discovered, could in any case be solved with little loss of performance by dropping the original 9.9:1 compression to the 8.3:1 previously standardized for the pushrod cars, and retained as an option for the Mark II on some overseas markets where the quality of fuel was still doubtful.

Maximum torque was substantially increased by 10 lb ft at the same rpm level, and to counter an occasional complaint that the MGA was fussy at high touring speeds, the final-drive ratio was changed to 4.1:1. This meant that at, say, 4500 rpm in top gear the Mark II would do 80.55 mph instead of the 76.5 of its predecessor, but it also caused some disappointment because the improved engine therefore provided a smaller improvement in acceleration than some people expected.

The car might have enjoyed a better reception if the stylists' work had matched that of the engineers, for the recessed front grille could scarcely be called a touch of genius, and the new tail-lights—which were in fact Mini lights mounted sideways—

quarrelled violently with the rear wing line instead of complementing it, as the previous tail-lights had done. However, it was a good idea to put black Vynide not only on the instrument panel, but also on the scuttle-top, to avoid having the body colour reflected in the windscreen glass.

In a somewhat grouchy road-test report, *Autocar* picked holes in most aspects of the Mark II and described the improvement in performance as 'marginal'. The figures quoted supported this, each step in the acceleration table being just about half-a-second better than before—but they did mention in passing that the engine of the car tested was 'barely run in'. When *Autocourse* tested the same car more than six months later, their figures were very different; the improvement ranged from 0.5 sec (0 to 30 mph) to 3.2 sec (0 to 80 mph).

Five-and-a-half years after greeting the MGA's roadholding and steering as being 'of a very high order' and adding 'There was no feeling of discomfort on *pavé* and other poor surfaces', *Autocar* decided that 'In many ways the ride, steering and roadholding of the MGA are very similar to those of a vintage sports car. . . . On all but smooth surfaces there are short, sharp up and down movements of the car'. Since the MGA's suspension had not changed, it was fairly obvious that *Autocar*'s criteria had. Instead of noting that the MGA now had built-in anchorages for seat belts, the magazine said disapprovingly: 'No seat belts were fitted on the car submitted for test'. The concluding sentence read: 'Basically, the MGA's traditional character, which has appealed to so many, is unchanged'. It left the reader in no doubt that to this magazine, at any rate, the attractions of the MGA no longer made any appeal.

World sales figures told the same sad story. It was time for the MGA to be replaced by a new, softer sports car called MGB.

A comparison of the rear lights standardized on the MGA 1500, MGA 1600, and MGA 1600 Mark II

The 100,000th MGA was a 1600 Mark II, seen here at the end of the production line. It was built to US specification and finished in gold metallic paint. Not unduly impressed, the American importers painted it over again

Chapter 4
MGA in competitions

When it was decided, late in 1954, that the British Motor Corporation should have its own competitions department, based at Abingdon, the man chosen to set it up was a benign individual named Marcus Chambers, then in his mid-forties. He had been part of the British motor sporting scene since long before World War 2 (during which he served in the RNVR), and had driven everything from tiny Austin Sevens to massive vintage Bentleys and a still more massive 7-litre 1907 Renault. Having successfully raced HRGs at Le Mans in 1937/38 and been chief mechanic to the same team 10 years later, he had earned the rare distinction of qualifying for membership of both the British Racing Drivers' Club *and* the British Racing Mechanics' Club.

After years of Continental travelling, Marcus could detect a Michelin rosette from a range of 25 kilometres, and a three-rosette establishment from the far side of an Alp. This expertise developed a well-rounded figure which earned him the nickname of 'Chubby' (usually abbreviated to Chub), alternating during his BMC period with that of 'The Poor Man's Neubauer', while in deference to his naval career the big Wolseleys used as rally service cars were known as the Admiral's Barges.

Pat Moss once remarked that, to her, Marcus was like a favourite uncle. To me he was equally kind,

'Marcus was like a favourite uncle.' Pat Moss with BMC's first competitions manager, Marcus Chambers, at a luncheon party celebrating some of their successes

and for a time my family shared the cottage where the Chambers family lived in a village south of Abingdon. That being so, it embarrasses me to record the simple fact that the MGA never won a major race or rally, for its production life coincided almost exactly with Marcus's management of the BMC Competitions Department.

As an intelligent man, Marcus knew the cars at his disposal in 1954/55 were incapable of winning an international event by reason of various deficiencies, whether of roadholding, braking, acceleration, speed, or all four together. He was perhaps less aware that if the cars had been better, very few of the BMC drivers had the ability to use them to the full. Or perhaps he *was* aware of this weakness in the team, but insufficiently ruthless to dispose of the amateurs and hangers-on as quickly as he he should have done. His successor, Stuart Turner, had no such qualms, and the BMC Competitions Department became the most successful organization of its

David Ash's 1956 Sebring MGA briefly leads Steve Spitler's car in an SCCA event at Cumberland, Maryland. In 1956 and 1957, these two and another MGA took the team prize in the Sebring 12 Hours in Florida

kind in the world—but it is Marcus Chambers who deserves the credit for laying a sound foundation for success as soon as good cars (and, therefore, good drivers) became available.

The disasters at Le Mans and Dundrod could have ended the MGA's competitions career before it had properly started. Certainly they caused BMC to concentrate (officially, at least) on rallies rather than races, and this was an additional problem in the early days, for the 'Comps' workshop was then controlled by Alec Hounslow, who was also foreman of Syd Enever's Development shop. Alec's main claim to fame (apart from an awe-inspiring capacity for draught beer) was his ride with Nuvolari in the 1933 Ulster TT-winning K3 Magnette, and he shared with Syd Enever a great love of speed events—whether races or record runs—combined with immense contempt for the rally world.

Plans had been made to run the Le Mans MGAs in the 1955 Alpine Rally, but the event was

cancelled in the furore following the Le Mans tragedy, so Marcus arranged a proving run on the Continent with an Austin A90, a Le Mans-engined A50 and one of the Le Mans MGAs. He also took a selection of BMC models to Montlhéry a few days after the new MGA was unveiled to the British public at the London Motor Show in October. In shocking weather conditions, and complete with hood and sidescreens, a fairly standard MGA 1500 put 102.54 miles into the hour driven by Ken Wharton. Alec Hounslow then stripped the car of its weather equipment, bumpers and so forth, fitted a

One of the Fitzwilliam/Carnegie team's MGAs in the 1957 Mille Miglia, when Carnegie returned the best British performance in the last of these classic 1000-mile Italian road races. This car also won the 1956 Autosport *production sports car championship*

DUNLOP
UMO 94

Ted Lund and Colin Escott test two hardtop Twin Cams for Sebring 1960, the model's second and last attempt at the Florida race

Intended originally as a truly competitive sports/racer, the Twin Cam would have been up against this kind of specialized machinery by the late 1950s

Le Mans 3.7:1 final drive, and in this form the MGA recorded 112.36 miles in the hour driven by John Gott, who said that on the straights the car was hitting 120 mph at about 5700 rpm.

Meanwhile a team of MGAs was being prepared for the all-important Sebring 12 Hours, because, whatever BMC felt about racing, it was necessary that the new MG should perform well in the 1956 Florida event to aid its acceptance in Abingdon's most significant market. Driven by Kinchloe/Spitler, Ash/Ehrman and Allen/Van Driel, the MGAs were of course outpaced by the works Porsches but finished the race intact to win the team prize. The following year, the Abingdon cars again took the team prize, also gaining first and second place in their class, although their overall placings in the race were lower.

A month after the 1956 Sebring race, however, Marcus had rather surprisingly entered two MGAs for the Mille Miglia. Once again they were, predictably, unable to match the performance of the Porsches, but the car driven into a humble 70th position by Peter Scott-Russell and Tom Haig was, in fact, the highest-placed British entry, despite the challenge of works HWM, Austin-Healeys, Triumph TR2s and ERA-prepared Sunbeam Rapiers. As at Sebring, the Mille Miglia performance was repeated in 1957, this time with privately-owned (but in some cases ex-works) cars. Robin Carnegie achieved an excellent 31st place overall, averaging 76.79 mph over the 1000 miles to beat all other British cars entered, while Hogg/Jones and Reid/Sparrowe took second and third places in one of the limited-price classes. Carnegie and Dick Fitzwilliam had won the *Autosport* Series Production Sports Car Championship with their MGA in 1956, and formed an MGA racing team for 1957, but Fitzwilliam's 1957 Mille Miglia came to an abrupt end when he hit a tree.

Insofar as any BMC plan emerges at this time, it was to stay out of racing—apart from preparing cars for Sebring and giving fairly generous assistance to selected private owners—and enter the works MGAs in those international rallies where they might be expected to achieve something, at least, while waiting a seemingly interminable time for the higher-performance Twin Cam to become available. And some quite reasonable results were achieved. The MGAs came 13th, 14th and 26th in the 1956 Liége–Rome–Liége, John Gott and Chris Tooley giving the best British performance in the event. In 1957 Gott was 14th overall and in 1958 he came 9th, earning a sought-after Prix Triennial, driving the first Twin Cam officially entered by BMC for an international rally. Meanwhile Nancy Mitchell—who had finished 74th in the 1956 Millie Miglia with her works MGA—performed consistently enough with MGAs and Magnettes to gain the Ladies' European Touring Championship twice running, in 1956 and 1957. And in the 1957 Acropolis Rally, two Greeks named Papadoupoulos and Politis surprised everybody by driving their own MGA 1500 into fifth place overall.

Despite all this, it gradually became clear that the MGA had already missed the boat in international rallies. When the Austin-Healey 100-Six came out in September 1956, 'Comps' recognized its potential and set about developing it into a rally-winner. As Marcus Chambers later remarked: 'We had long felt that we needed a car with long, hairy legs to stride over the mountains and great lungs with which to rush up the hills; this seemed to be it.' That brilliant pair, Pat Moss and Ann Wisdom, took to the big Healey immediately, and when it grew into the Austin-Healey 3000 in 1959, they soon showed the rally world what they could do. Once content with such meagre pickings as team prizes and ladies' awards accompanied by 20th or 30th place overall, the BMC team now began to taste the delights of outright victory in the world's toughest international events.

In fairness to the MGA, however, it must be said—and I say it from personal experience—that the works-prepared big Healeys behaved very differently from the production version, which in turn differed considerably from the MGA. Although the Austin-Healey and the MGA were built in the same factory, the design policies that had brought the two cars into being were not at all the same, for in one case performance was allowed to take precedence over roadholding, and in the other the reverse was true. The MG approach was explained in detail by John Thornley in the second edition of his book, *Maintaining the Breed*: 'For years, MGs had been built under the slogan "Safety Fast"—and this, at Abingdon, was regarded as no empty phrase but rather as a challenge. A car could easily be built which was too fast for its own inherent stability.... The new car would have a maximum speed of the order of 100 mph and some would be bought by tyro drivers. Above all, therefore, the new car had to be stable. The designers' brief was to make a car which was, first and foremost, "safe" as defined above; which, secondly, was at least as rugged, as well-appointed and well-finished as its predecessors; and thirdly, was to sell as nearly as possible at the price of the TF. Only then were speed and acceleration to be considered.

'The above sequence is important. It underlies the confidence in the future success of the car, and of its continued acceptance by a discriminating public. It is *not*, be it admitted, a prescription which wins races—the more is the pity—but for every owner who wishes to go motor racing, there are a hundred

Dick Jacobs, proprietor of Mill Garage on the outskirts of London, ran two Twin Cams with considerable success in sports car racing

63
63
IMTW

64
64
2MTW

and more who do not.

At the time those words were written, the Twin Cam version of the MGA did not exist, but one of the prototype engines was about to be installed in the EX179 record car for a successful Utah run at more than 170 mph. It was therefore a fairly open secret in the mid-1950s that although Abingdon recognized the limitations of the pushrod MGA 1500 as a competition car, the factory hoped to market an additional model that would be competitive in major rallies and sports car races. Unfortunately for such ambitions, this was a period of rapid development in sports-racing, and by the time the MGA Twin Cam finally got into production, all the genuine roadgoing sports cars in the 1500 and 1600 cc categories had been completely outclassed by Elva, Tojeiro, Cooper, Lotus and the like. In international rallying, as already mentioned, the big Healey clearly offered more chance of success once its chassis had been 'sorted'. To add insult to injury, even the Frogeye Sprite—announced a couple of months before the Twin Cam—had the makings of a more successful competition car by virtue of its small size, nimble handling and ready response to extensive tuning.

Because the Twin Cam was not ready in time for Sebring 1958, no MGAs were entered and the team prize was taken by BMC's trio of Austin-Healeys. As mentioned earlier, the new model made its rally debut as an official BMC entry in the Liége–Rome–Liége, which was held at the end of August. Although announced in mid-July, the Twin Cam was not available to ordinary mortals for quite some time and therefore missed most of the 1958 season. However, Dick Jacobs secured one for Foster and Bridger to drive in the Tourist Trophy, now run at Goodwood and held in mid-September, and with a 76.2 mph average for the 4-hour race the lone Twin Cam reached 14th place overall, third in

The Jacobs Twin Cams in action, driven by Alan Foster (1 MTW) and Roy Bloxam (2 MTW). In this, the 1959 Oulton Park Gold Cup Race, Foster won his class but 2 MTW threw a connecting-rod

In 1959 a syndicate of MGCC members ran a Twin Cam roadster at Le Mans, where it performed well until an encounter with a dog damaged the front, causing eventual retirement from overheating. Rebuilt as a 1762 cc coupé, it did very well to win the 2-litre class in 1960. After the race it was driven home to Lancashire, and in 1961 competed a third time, but failed to finish

the 2-litre class behind the factory Porsche 1500 RSKs, which were fourth and eighth in general classification. It was quite a respectable performance for what Gregor Grant of *Autosport* called 'probably the only genuine production car in the race'. However, that magazine's 3-hour race at Snetterton in October saw the Twin Cams outpaced by K. W. Mackenzie's pushrod 1500, which won its class with third place overall at 73.09 mph average.

As things turned out, the Abingdon-built Twin Cams ran twice only at Sebring. In 1959, Saidel/Ehrman and Dalton/Parkinson took second and third places in their class, but the third car had to be pushed over the finish line. In fact all three had experienced trouble of one sort or another, and the team prize was won by three Sprites. In 1960 the cars again gave trouble and one retired, although the remaining two were third and fourth in class, driven by Hayes/Leavens and Parkinson/Flaherty. With 24th place overall at 68.5 mph, the faster of the survivors had proved slower than the works Sprites,

John Gott and Ray Brookes drove a Twin Cam coupé in the 1959 Monte Carlo Rally, but crashed during the mountain section

12

11
151

and Marcus Chambers came home thoroughly disgusted with the behaviour of his cars.

Marcus was now turning to the Austin-Healey 3000 as his ideal rally car. In the 1959 Monte, one Twin Cam was entered for John Gott to drive, but he slid off the road at an icy stretch of the mountain test. In the Tulip Rally, Gott's Twin Cam was penalized for a navigational error, and John Sprinzel crashed his at Zandvoort. In the Acropolis Rally, Sprinzel again drove a Twin Cam, and again crashed, leaving a couple of privately-owned 1500s to take second and third places in their class.

The most consistently successful Twin Cams in competitions were, of course, Dick Jacobs's two, 1 MTW and 2 MTW. During the winter of 1958/59, Dick had both cars stripped completely and lightened wherever possible, using aluminium instead of steel for unstressed body parts, fitting lighter seats and lightweight batteries—to such effect that the finished cars were more than 250 lb lighter than the 1958 TT car had been. Both engines were meticulously prepared, balanced and fairly mildly tuned, while the fuel-starvation bogey was countered by fitting larger pumps and pipes, which gave 38 gph instead of the normal flow of only 15 gph.

Early in the 1959 racing season, the two cars were driven by Roy Bloxam and Alan Foster into a class first and second in the Silverstone GT race ahead of two other Twin Cams, Foster returning an 82.97 mph lap-time which remained a class record for two years. Unlike most of their competitors, the two Twin Cams were usually driven to each race instead of being trailered—and normally driven back home afterwards, for they seldom failed to finish. After each event, Dick's garage checked the top end of one engine, and the bottom end of the other, and at the end of the season he would send me a summary of their achievements for use in the BMC sports car magazine, *Safety Fast*.

Opposite, top *Another unsuccessful Twin Cam attempt was made by John Sprinzel and Dick Bensted-Smith, who crashed in the 1959 Acropolis Rally. However, privately-owned MGAs came second and third in class*

Opposite, below *The MGA's last production year brought two notable successes for 151 ABL, a works-built Mark II De Luxe. After a classwin scored by the Morley brothers in the 1962 Monte, it had no more than an oilchange and checkover before gaining another classwin in Holland's Tulip Rally. Crewed by Rauno Aaltonen and Tony Ambrose, it made the fastest Col de Turini climb of the entire entry regardless of engine size*

In 1959 and again in 1960 the cars (usually both together) were entered for 16 events, gaining a total of 32 class or overall 'places', twice winning their class in the *Autosport* Championship, and in 1960 repeating the class third of two years earlier in the TT at Goodwood. For the 1960 season the cars had been modified slightly more, but in the entire year only two retirements (one from fuel starvation, one with a burst tyre) were recorded. Indeed, the driver who subsequently bought 2 MTW used it for a time as a shopping car!

The reliability of these Twin Cams was, of course,

For Sebring 1961, MG entered two pushrod 1600 Mark I coupés. Flaherty/Parkinson (44) came 14th and Riley/Whitmore (43) were 16th overall, taking first and second places in their class

a direct result of the superb preparation and maintenance they received at Dick Jacobs's hands, and he asked comparatively little of Abingdon during this time. Others were somewhat more demanding. Backed by a syndicate of MG Car Club members, Ted Lund—like Dick Jacobs, one of the original MGA Le Mans team—asked if Enever would build him a Twin Cam to drive at Le Mans in 1959. The car was duly prepared, taken to Le Mans, and ran well until Lund's co-driver, Colin Escott, had the misfortune to hit an Alsatian dog when travelling at well over 100 mph. Although he was able to continue, the crumpled bodywork caused the gearbox to overheat so much that eventually it seized up, and the Twin Cam retired after some 19 hours' running.

As Marcus Chambers flags the classwinning MGA to a routine stop at Sebring 1961, he demonstrates why he was nicknamed 'the poor man's Neubauer'. . .

For the following year the car was rebuilt as an odd-looking fixed-head coupé, with engine opened out to 1762 cc. Although this put it in the 2-litre class with the Porsches, Triumphs and AC-Bristols, Lund and Escott averaged a most creditable 91.12 mph to win the class, finishing 12th overall—and Ted then drove it home to his native Lancashire. Fired by this success, Abingdon's Development workshop evolved a really exciting Twin Cam which looked like a scaled-down D type Jaguar, complete with head-fairing, but had to dispose of it surreptitiously to avoid big trouble with BMC's management. In its place, the 1960 coupé ran in the 1961 Le Mans race but succumbed to engine trouble.

Meanwhile MG had to do something about that other (and commercially more important) long-distance race, the Sebring 12 Hours. Two handsome and purposeful-looking coupés were built on Twin Cam chassis, with well-prepared pushrod 1600 engines, and shipped to Florida. There the thermometer was hovering around the 85-degree mark, so the partially-blanked front grilles came in for some attention during practice, and the 1600s ran nicely

Three 1622 cc De Luxe coupés finished the 1962 Sebring race, but without gaining an award. Comparison with the 1960 and 1961 cars shows the effort needed to keep drivers and engines cool in the Florida heat

JAGUAR
Gulfpride
ALITALIA

throughout the 1961 race to finish first and second in their class, driven by Parkinson/Flaherty and Riley/Whitmore, beating the works Elvas and Sunbeam Alpines. Three similar cars, with 1622 cc engines, gap-toothed front grilles and shallower front aprons, were built for the 1962 race. They completed the 12-hour event in 16th, 17th and 20th places overall, but without gaining an award in this, the MGA's last appearance at Sebring.

The potential of the 1622 cc De Luxe coupé was underlined during the MGA's last production year by the performance of 151 ABL, built by 'Comps' for the 1962 Monte Carlo Rally. To the Morley brothers, Don and Erle, it must have seemed a very mild device after the much-modified Healeys they usually drove for BMC, but they took it through from Oslo in fine style to win the 2-litre class. This earned an approving nod from Stuart Turner, who had succeeded Marcus Chambers as Competitions Manager in October 1961, and he invited one of his newest recruits, Rauno Aaltonen, to drive the same car in the Tulip Rally, partnered by that highly experienced navigator, Tony Ambrose. With two big Healeys to prepare for the Dutch event, not to mention the Mini-Cooper with which Pat Moss won it outright, 151 ABL was given no more attention than a clean-up, checkover and oil-change after the Monte Carlo Rally. This did not deter Aaltonen from beating all the works TR4s to win his class. The Tulip Rally being a handicap event, only those on the spot felt the full impact of Rauno's drive, in the course of which he made the fastest Col de Turini climb *of the entire entry*, 13 sec faster than the Austin-Healey 3000 and E type Jaguar which tied for second best performance on that section. Three years later the young Finn was to become European Rally Champion, driving the Mini-Coopers which had made all other BMC cars obsolete as successful contenders in international rallying.

Chapter 5
Personal view

At first sight I rather disliked the MGA, having grown up with angular sports cars, and I wasn't too impressed when I later drove one for the first time. This may have been because in those days I was ghosting road-test reports for a famous racing driver, and therefore encountering many expensive and/or exotic vehicles. Moreover, one of the tricks of that trade is to make snap judgements on a car, concealing the fact that (a) you may have driven it no more than five miles, and (b) the Famous Racing Driver may not have driven it at all.

In February 1959 I started work at Abingdon to produce a new BMC sports car magazine. My boss, John Thornley, said with characteristic understanding: 'If you're writing about our cars, you'd better find out what they're like,' and arranged for one or other of the press demonstrators to be put at my disposal every weekend. For the first time I had the chance to drive substantial distances in good, fast cars: Austin-Healey 100-Six and 3000, MGA 1500, Twin Cam, and from mid-1959 onwards the MGA 1600. It was heaven.

Britain was a different world for motorists then. There were no motorways, but no overall speed limits either, and no sneaky radar traps in the towns. By present standards the roads seemed almost empty, except for a few slow lorries and a sprinkling of underpowered family cars, mostly incapable of cornering fast and seldom driven at more than 40 mph even on the straight. In a good sports car one could and did make rings around them, savouring the acceleration, braking and roadholding that made this possible. On such roads a respectable cross-country average was a challenge and a joy, in no way resembling today's tedious motorway grind with one eye on the road ahead and one on the rear-view mirror.

Early in 1960 came the chance to attend a three-day racing school at Montlhéry. I had not raced for more than a decade, and assumed the school training would be a fairly mild-mannered affair, so I set off for Paris in a bog-standard MGA 1600 press car with 48-spoke wheels and 'cooking' Dunlops (probably the old crossply Gold Seals).

Mild it wasn't. Before the second day ended, one hand was blistered from gear-changing (my glove

As described in the text, an MGA 1600 press car was used for the three-day racing school at Montlhéry in 1960 and performed well, apart from trouble with the 48-spoke wire wheels

having split on the first afternoon), and on the third morning of the course the scrutineers hesitated to pass the MGA because its tyres were almost bald. The school had attracted about 150 pupils from all over the Continent, including an unknown Swiss youngster called Jo Siffert, and our instructors were Paul Frère and Willy Daetwyler, one-time hillclimb champion of Europe. Among the two dozen cars in the 1600 class were no less than 19 Porsches, mostly 1600S models, plus a Super 90 and a Carrera. In such company I was content to be placed ninth, my 48-spoke wheels quietly disintegrating on the Montlhéry road circuit. They lasted long enough to get me back to Abingdon, where a shocked Press Department workshop took all five wheels and tyres and threw them away. The rest of the car was in fine shape.

This excursion sharpened the urge to go racing again—which seemed impossible, as I had no suitable car and no money. Gordon Cobban, then honorary secretary of the MGCC South-Eastern Centre (and eventually my successor as the Club's general secretary when BL withdrew works backing), solved the problem by generously offering an occasional drive in the MGA 1500 he used for speed events. Later he was persuaded to let me prepare the car as well; I would have to do this at home to save money, but obviously I had access to factory know-how and could buy cheaply or scrounge most of the necessary bits.

What followed may be of interest, if only to demonstrate the law of diminishing returns as applied to motor racing. Gordon's car, VPO 320, was a near-standard 1956 MGA with gas-flowed head, Alexander camshaft, and front brakes converted to discs. On standard carburettors it would do about 6500 rpm in the indirect gears, but the valve timing limited its top-gear performance, and the unmodified bottom end lacked stamina for racing. I picked up some class awards in my first four sprints, but on my first Silverstone outing a big-end went after five laps, though I had not bettered 86.2 sec (about 67 mph average).

We seized the opportunity to fit a 1600 engine with lightened flywheel, competition clutch, Twin Cam rods, high-compression (9.75:1) pistons, Twin Cam carburettors on the AEH200 manifold, but a standard MGA camshaft and the same head as before. The Le Mans close-ratio gears and a 4.55:1 axle proved just right for the short Silverstone circuit (conveniently close to Abingdon, which saved hotel costs), and I had an oldish set of Dunlop R5 racing tyres to use in the dry, plus a set of Magnette wheels shod with Durabands for wet-weather wear.

Next time out at Silverstone showed a lap-time improvement to 81.8 sec, despite fuel-pump trouble which limited top-gear rpm to only 5000, and put me out of a scratch 10-lapper when leading. After fitting a bigger pump from a Healey I could see 6000 rpm on the straight, but no more. The car was now slightly faster and definitely more reliable, giving me a good hour-and-a-half stint for the MGA team in the National 6-Hour Relay Race, but the change to 1600 cc put me in the same class as the Twin Cams. The fastest of these were then lapping Silverstone in 74 sec, just over 78 mph average, and faster than John Gott's Austin-Healey 3000. Only when the Twin Cams were racing elsewhere did any silverware come my way.

So the decision was made to rebuild the other engine and return to the 1500 cc class, compensating for the smaller capacity by lightening the car where possible. This process was limited by the need to return the car to road trim eventually, as it was still Gordon's property. In effect, he allowed me to remove anything I liked, provided I did so with a spanner instead of a saw. I took off the front grille, front apron, the hood, the passenger's seat and most of the interior trim. The standard batteries were replaced by a gnat-sized device fitted in the space normally occupied by the heater. The pukka 'Brooklands' aero screen gave way to a homemade plastic job weighing far less. I remade the plywood floorboards in aluminium, taping the half tonneau-cover in place to stop people climbing in and falling through the 22 SWG floor. When I'd finished, the unfortunate MGA was extremely ugly but far

The author greets Stuart Seager (his assistant editor in the early 1960s), who was taking pictures during the Six-Hour Relay at Silverstone in 1961. VPO 320 had at this time a tuned 1600 cc engine and fairly standard bodywork

lighter (much of it being now stashed away in my garage).

The 1500 engine was rebuilt with 713/12 Sebring camshaft and matching distributor, larger (Mark II) exhaust valves, and handpicked springs of carefully equalized installed length. The inlet manifold was mated to the head and pegged. I fitted a lock-out screw on the gearbox to avoid hitting reverse when changing into second for a tight right-hander, and reduced inside wheel lift (which was limiting usable acceleration) by modifying the rear springs and lengthening the check straps.

My first 1962 Silverstone meeting allowed no direct comparisons because it poured most of the day, but our three-car team came third in the David Brown Relay Race, and in a later half-hour event I came fourth behind a Lola, a Lotus Seven and a TR3. I had seen an easy 6500 in the gears and 6400 (exactly 110 mph) in top, but with a tendency to lose speed on the straight. Development Department

This picture, taken on the approach to Silverstone's Woodcote Corner, shows how VPO 320 measured up to the opposition after suitable modification. There was no difficulty in winning this race, for instance

diagnosed fuel starvation due to float-chamber frothing, so I fitted the carburettors on anti-vibration mountings, and a double pump to be on the safe side. Three weeks later at the MGCC Silverstone meeting, everything came right: five awards in five events, the fastest race-winning average of the day, and a lap in 79.8 secs—within 0.2 secs of the fastest lap of the day (by a Twin Cam, of course!).

Three weeks after that, I was driving up to Silverstone for yet another meeting when, just north of Oxford, I heard a funny noise as I took top at 5500 rpm. Under the bonnet I found half a sparking-plug insulator swinging by its HT lead; under the car I found a mysterious bulge in the sump.

The crankshaft breakage was hardly surprising. I had started using 6600 in the gears and, in the heat of the moment, had once touched 7000 in third. The vibration was so bad that when changing gear, it

Overleaf *Rebuilt as a much-lightened 1500 to avoid the faster Twin Cams in the 1600 cc class, VPO 320 took many awards during 1962*

SUPER
PLUS

SUPER-PLUS
JOHN
56
849 WPB
41

Above *Taken just after flagfall at Silverstone, this shot illustrates the difference between standard and close-ratio gears in the MGA. The second and fourth cars have the edge on initial getaway with standard gearboxes. With close-ratio gears, the first and third cars are at first handicapped by their higher bottom gear—but they made it first to Copse Corner*

Opposite *Another shot of VPO 320 in finally developed form, with extensive lightening and partly-stripped interior. The car was raced with taped half-tonneau cover in the days before crash-bars, using a Microcell bucket seat and hoping the lap-strap would permit ducking into the cockpit if things went seriously wrong*

was rather a matter of choosing which of the half-dozen gear-levers to grab. The root of the trouble was the MGA's lug-drive clutch, which tended to go out of concentricity and therefore unbalanced, unlike the Hausermann strap-drive clutch of the MGB. Too late I learned that the fastest Twin Cam operators fitted a new clutch every two or three races. So once again I rebuilt the engine with a new crankshaft, connecting rods, pistons, clutch, timing chain, oil cooler and heavens knows what else. At the same time I fitted an MGB twin exhaust manifold, a fibreglass transmission tunnel, lighter fibreglass seats, and a set of fibreglass wings. The wings bled through pink every time they were sprayed white, so we gave up and painted the whole car red—a colour I much dislike.

How VPO would have performed in this guise I cannot say. A family bereavement ended my racing plans in mid-season, and with the MGB shortly due for announcement it was time for Gordon to sell the

MG
YRX 983

old warhorse. It was bought by a young man, very impressed by the car's considerable racing reputation, who refitted all the road equipment and never drove it on a racetrack.

It had taken some two years of concentrated effort to trim the car's Silverstone lap-time by 6.4 seconds. Was it worth it? I thought so when I was holding an armful of trophies at the MGCC annual dinner, but now—well, I don't know. . . .

Meanwhile, with the MGB coming soon, Syd Enever had some Development Department MGAs to dispose of. My choice fell on EX191/273, a car with a complicated history. The bodyshell was very early 1500 with a cutaway at the front where a Twin Cam engine had once been installed, some filled-in holes at the back where it had once had independent rear suspension, and deeply-scored 'ten lines' in the paintwork—a relic of tests on MIRA *pavé*. The chassis was brand-new 1600 Mark II, with disc wheels. 'Why do you want the tattiest car in the shop?', asked Syd. Quite simply, because I knew it would be cheap and it was the perfect basis for the car I wanted: my ideal MGA.

The new running gear would of course be unworn, and I preferred disc to wire wheels after my Montlhéry experience. The Mark II frame would even have seat-belt anchorages. The car had always run on 'trade' plates, so it had yet to be registered—giving me a 1961 MGA at a 1955 price. It would have to be painted, so I could make various changes first, then choose my own colour.

First I had the rear deck cut away to the hood line, MGB style, to provide more space at the back of the cockpit. An MG Midget locking handle on the trunk lid gave a secure luggage space, increased if necessary by putting the spare wheel on an external luggage grid. I had MGA 1600 sidelights at the front, sealed-beam headlamps, and old-style MGA 1500 tail-lights with separate flashers mounted on the

Previous page *The two MGAs driven most by the author, for road and track use. Much lightened without changing the front suspension setting, the 'racer' sits much higher and needed more development in this respect, but it was strictly a low-budget tuning programme!*

body. The front grille was 1500/1600 instead of Mark II, and the MGB-type scuttle grille (leftover from some other Enever experiment) served to confuse people, if nothing else. The paint job I chose was a dark smoky grey, because I believed (as I still believe) that a dark-coloured car can be driven anything between 10 and 20 mph faster without arousing unwelcome attention from men in peaked caps. A pair of Microcell bucket seats, quite steeply raked, gave good all-round support and, together with a shortened steering column, provided a reasonably straight-arm driving position, with the gear-lever modified to keep it comfortably within reach.

So far from tuning the 1622 cc engine I detuned it, if anything, by fitting a special camshaft that gave better middle-range acceleration without losing much at the top end. Again sacrificing maximum speed to acceleration, I chose the old 1500/1600 axle ratio of 4.3:1 instead of the Mark II's 4.1. Into the gearbox casing (the nicely-ribbed and rigid Mark II version) went a set of Le Mans close-ratio gears—the only ones I really liked—which gave an evenly-spaced 40, 60, 80 and 100 mph in the four gears. The headlamps were dipped by a lever instead of a foot-switch, so that I could dip and change gear simultaneously on twisty roads after dark, and I found room on the dash-panel to fit a small ammeter.

I had never much liked the MGA coupé, which to me looked like a reluctantly-tamed two-seater wearing a small bowler hat, but for my own car I eventually scrounged a hardtop which was used in winter, so as to provide a measure of extra comfort and incidentally make the folding top last longer by protecting it from the cold weather.

YRX 983 was bought late in 1961, and stayed with me until early in 1964, when I took on a new publicity job that brought with it a company car. It proved to be exactly what I wanted: a taut little sports car which was comfortable for long journeys, with reasonable (and lockable) luggage space plus extra stowage behind the seats, and the opportunity to enjoy top-down motoring in the right weather conditions. By the standards of 20-odd years ago the roadholding, brakes and acceleration were excellent, and the car was engineered in such a way that its performance could always be used to the full.

Above all, my 'ideal' MGA had that special MGA quality of being fun to drive, differing from other MGAs only in the fact that, to me, it was even more enjoyable than they were. When I sold YRX I missed her more than I could have imagined. A couple of years later, when she came on the market again, I was sorely tempted to buy her back again.

Specifications

MGA 1500

Production period	August 1955 to May 1959
Cars built	58,750
ENGINE	
	Four-cylinder with cast-iron block/crankcase and cast-iron cylinder head. Three-bearing crankshaft. Clamp-type small ends to connecting-rods. Lubrication by eccentric-rotor pump, with full-flow external filter. Pushrod-operated overhead valves
Bore, stroke & capacity	73.03 × 88.9 mm = 1489 cc
Compression ratio	8.3:1
Max power & torque	72 bhp (53.85 Kw) at 5500 rpm net. Early cars, 68 bhp (50.86 Kw) 77.4 lb ft (106.81 Nm) at 3500 rpm
Fuel system	Twin SU semi-downdraught 1.5 in. carburettors. Rear-mounted SU electric fuel pump. Tank capacity = 10 Imp gallons (12 US gallons, 45.5 litres)
TRANSMISSION	
	Single plate 8-in dry clutch with hydraulic actuation. Four-speed manual gearbox with remote control, ratios 4.76 (R), 3.64, 2.21, 1.37 and 1:1. Open propeller shaft with needle-bearing universal joints. Hypoid bevel final drive, ratio 4.3:1
CHASSIS	Separate box-section frame with braced bulkhead and tubular cross-members. Independent front suspension by coil spring and wishbone. Non-independent rear suspension with semi-elliptic leaf springs. Lever-arm hydraulic dampers. Rack-and-pinion steering

Brakes	Lockheed hydraulically-actuated drum brakes, front and rear, diameter = 10 in. Single master cylinder without servo assistance
Wheels & tyres	Four-stud pressed-steel disc wheels with 5.60 × 15 in. tyres on 4J rims. Option of centrelock wire-spoked wheels
Electrical	12-volt Lucas positive-earth system with DC generator and two 6-volt batteries in series. Coil ignition with vacuum/centrifugal advance on contact-breaker. Prefocus double-dip headlamps, 42/36 watt
DIMENSIONS	Wheelbase = 94 in. (2388 mm) Front track (discs) = 47.5 in. (1207 mm) (wires) = 47.88 in. (1216 mm) Rear track (discs) = 48.75 in. (1238 mm) (wires) = 48.75 in. (1238 mm)
	Length = 156 in. (3962 mm) Width = 58 in. (1473 mm) Height = 50 in. (1270 mm)
Quoted kerb weight	1980 lb (900 Kg) approximately

Additional options include radio, heater, adjustable steering column, tonneau cover, badge bar, luggage grid, 4.55:1 final drive, hardtop, etc

MGA TWIN CAM

Production period	April 1958 to April 1960
Cars built	2111
ENGINE	Basically as MGA 1500 but 75.4 × 88.9 mm (1588 cc), with aluminium alloy cylinder head, fully-floating gudgeon pins, and overhead camshafts driven by duplex chain and bearing on shim-adjusted inverted-bucket tappets. Remote header tank to radiator. Compression ratio, 9.9:1
Max power & torque	107 bhp (80.03 Kw) at 6500 rpm net 104 lb ft (143.52 Nm) at 4500 rpm
Fuel system	Twin SU semi-downdraught 1.75 in. carburettors. Larger-capacity fuel pump
TRANSMISSION	As MGA 1500 but with optional close-ratio gearbox (2.44, 1.62, 1.27 and 1:1) and choice of five final-drive ratios (3.9, 4.3, 4.55, 4.875 and 5.125:1)

CHASSIS	As MGA 1500 but with Dunlop disc brakes front and rear, and peg-drive centrelock pressed-steel wheels. Tyres, 5.90 × 15 in. Dunlop Roadspeed
DIMENSIONS	Mainly as MGA 1500. Front track = 48 in. (1219 mm). Rear track = 48.88 in. (1242 mm)
Quoted kerb weight	2108 lb (956 Kg) approximately

Additional options include competition screen, light-alloy road wheels, oil cooler, anti-roll bar, limited-slip differential unit, long-range fuel tankage, higher-compression pistons, Weber carburettors or larger SU carburettors

MGA 1600 MARK I

Production period	May 1959 to April 1961
Cars built	31,501
ENGINE	As MGA 1500 but 75.4 × 88.9 mm (1588 cc)
Max power & torque	79.5 bhp (59.46 Kw) at 5600 rpm net 87 lb ft (120.06 Nm) at 3800 rpm
TRANSMISSION	As MGA 1500
CHASSIS	As MGA 1500 but with Lockheed 11 in. disc brakes at front
Electrical	As MGA 1500 but headlamps 50/40 watt
DIMENSIONS	As MGA 1500 but kerb weight = 2016 lb (916 Kg) approximately.

MGA 1600 MARK II

Production period	April 1961 to June 1962
Cars built	8719

ENGINE

Redesigned version of Mark I unit with new 76.2 × 88.9 mm (1622 cc) block, new crankshaft, rods and pistons, lighter flywheel, and new cylinder head with improved combustion chambers, better porting, larger valves and stronger springs

Compression ratio Choice of 8.9 or 8.3:1

Max power & torque 90 bhp (67.32 Kw) at 5500 rpm net
97 lb ft (133.86 Nm) at 4000 rpm

TRANSMISSION

Gearbox casing ribbed for extra rigidity. Final drive ratio = 4.1:1

CHASSIS

As MGA 1600 Mark I, but with seat-belt anchorages provided

Electrical Improved ignition distributor

DIMENSIONS As MGA 1600 Mark I

Production and export of all MGA models

	1955	1956	1957	1958	1959	1960	1961	1962	Totals
MGA 1500	793	12,611	19,805	15,431	7423	—	—	—	Export: 56,0
	210	799	766	691	221	—	—	—	Home: 2687
MGA Twin Cam	—	—	—	476	1242	33	—	—	Export: 1751
	—	—	—	65	277	18	—	—	Home: 360
MGA 1600 Mark I	—	—	—	—	13,235	15,776	318	—	Export: 29,3
	—	—	—	—	921	1154	97	—	Home: 2172
MGA 1600 Mark II	—	—	—	—	—	—	5185	2938	Export: 8123
	—	—	—	—	—	—	485	111	Home: 596
Annual production	1003	13,410	20,571	16,663	23,319	16,981	6085	3049	Total production: 101,081
Annual exports	793	12,611	19,805	15,907	21,900	15,809	5503	2938	Total exports: 95,2

Major MGA placings in international competitions, 1955 to 1962

1955

Le Mans 24 Hours Race: 5th and 6th in class (12th and 17th overall)
Tourist Trophy Race: 4th in class (20th overall)

1956

Sebring 12 Hours Race: Team Award (19th, 20th and 22nd overall)
Mille Miglia: Best British Performance (70th and 74th overall); 4th and 5th in class
Cape GP, South Africa: 1st overall
Autosport Production Sports Car Championship: 1st and 3rd overall
RAC Rally of Great Britain: 1, 2, 3 in class
Circuit of Ireland: Sports Car Team Award
RSAC Scottish Rally: 2nd in class; Winner, Ladies' Prize
Liége–Rome–Liége Rally: Best British Performance (13th, 14th and 26th overall); Runner-up, Ladies' Prize
Alpine Rally: 3, 4, 5 in GT Category; Winner, Ladies' Prize (15th overall)
Rally Ibérico, Portugal: 1st in class

1957

Sebring 12 Hours Race: 1st and 2nd in class plus Team Award (23rd, 27th and 36th overall)
Mille Miglia: Best British Performance (31st overall); 2nd and 3rd in class
Lyons-Charbonnières Rally: Ladies' Prize (32nd overall)
Acropolis Rally: 1st in class (5th overall)
Liége–Rome–Liége: Ladies Prize (16th overall). Also 14th overall

1958

Tulip Rally: 4th in class
Liége–Rome–Liége Rally: Prix Triennial and 9th overall
Tourist Trophy Race: 3rd in class (14th overall)
Autosport Three Hours: 3rd overall and 1st in class

1959

Sebring 12 Hours Race: 2nd and 3rd in class
Rand Nine Hours, South Africa: 3rd overall
Silverstone GT Race: 1, 2, 3 and 4 in class with record fastest lap
Pietermaritzburg Six Hours, South Africa: 2nd and 3rd overall (Index)
Autosport Championship: 1st in class
Circuit of Ireland: 3rd in class
Acropolis Rally: 2nd and 3rd in class

1960

Sebring 12 Hours Race: 3rd and 4th in class
Le Mans 24 Hours Race: 1st in class (12th overall)
Tourist Trophy Race: 3rd in class
Autosport Three Hours Race: 3rd overall and 1st in class
Autosport Championship: 1st and 2nd in class
Snetterton GT Race: 2nd and 3rd overall
Phoenix Park Handicap Race: 2nd and 3rd overall
Circuit of Ireland: 2nd in class
Deutschland Rally: 2nd in class

1961

Sebring 12 Hours Race: 1st and 2nd in class (14th and 16th overall)
Autosport Championship: 3rd overall
Zandvoort Sports Car Handicap, Holland: 1st overall
RAC Rally of Great Britain: 2nd in class
Scottish Rally Championship: 1st

1962

Sebring 12 Hours Race: No award (16th, 17th and 20th overall)
Monte Carlo Rally: 1st in class
Tulip Rally: 1st in class

Acknowledgements

As in the case of the earlier *MGB* AutoHistory, the source of this book is essentially the same as *MG by McComb* and the same acknowledgements would be reproduced here if space allowed. But it does not. It is also a sad but unavoidable fact that a great many of those who helped me in earlier days are no longer with us; we are the poorer for their passing.

John Thornley, Roy Brocklehurst, Gerald Palmer and Peter Morgan gave me valued assistance. It would be seemly, if a little overdue, to place on record my gratitude to Gordon Cobban for allowing me to race his MGA more than 20 years ago, and to those at Abingdon, BMC Engines Branch and elsewhere who tolerated my continual scrounging of special parts and tuning information.

That Nigel Smith's 1959 Twin Cam made the front cover is the measure of his ability as an amateur paint-sprayer and home mechanic. Peter Tipton of the MG Car Club helped me contact some of the owners who kindly provided pictures of their cars, or allowed my wife Caroline and myself to photograph them; we are sometimes unsure who took which picture, but as I can't draw, all special artwork is strictly her department. *Autosport* and *Motor* allowed reproduction of material from their back numbers, which, I think, provides an admirable picture of the period. If I add the names of Graham Gauld, George Phillips, Cyril Posthumus, Bill and Jenny Price, David Reynolds, Fred Scatley, Stuart Seager and Michael Ware, I hope that nobody has been overlooked . . . and offer my thanks and apologies to anyone who *has* been inadvertently left out.

F W McComb

Index